A JOURNEY WITH JESUS

A JOURNEY WITH JESUS

by
Tricia Craib

Illustrated by Graeme Hewitson

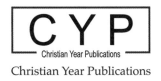

Christian Year Publications

ISBN-13: 978 1 912522 55 2

Copyright © 2019 by Christian Year Publications.
40 Beansburn, Kilmarnock, Scotland

Typeset by John Ritchie Ltd., Kilmarnock
Printed by Bell & Bain Ltd., Glasgow

Contents

Story 7 - Jesus The Healer

Story 8 - Life on the Road with Jesus

Story 9 - Jesus Shows His Love

Story 10 - It Is Finished

Story 11 - A Glorious Ending

Story 12 - Creation

Endorsements

'Tricia Craib's retellings are delivered with such warmth . . . freshly re-imagined, engaging the emotions and often very moving.'

Renita Boyle, author of:
Time for Bed Bible, Not a Cloud in the Sky and Tell it Together.
50 Bible Tell Togethers to Share

A Journey with Jesus is a collection of stories for children based on the life of Jesus. Tricia Craib uses her imagination to take readers right into the scene. Creating characters like Reuben and Sarah, members of the innkeeper's family, she begins with the account of Jesus' birth and then works through the Gospels introducing others, including Bible characters, in order to tell the Lord's story from their points of view. The book weaves through Christ's years on earth from His birth to His baptism, through His ministry to His death and resurrection. It concludes with her characters discussing why Jesus had to die and be raised again.

A Journey with Jesus is a book of stories about Bible stories as so much is included that is not in the Bible. The information that is there will, however, help its readers to understand the background to the Gospel account.

Irene Howat
Author of many different Christian biographies as well as multiple children's books

Dedication

For Caitlin, Erin and Megan Vernon who read the first draft of these stories and gave me some positive feedback.

Acknowledgements

Firstly I would like to thank all who helped and encouraged me to write these stories. I could not have produced this book without a lot of help from my friends and family especially my husband Kenny. I also thank my daughter Julie who inspired me to write the rest of the stories and complete the book. I am deeply grateful to my brother Norman and friends Anne Nicol, Meryl Pontin and Anne Wark for their hard work proof-reading the manuscript. I am also indebted to Graeme who was able to use some of my photos, taken in the Holy Land, as the background to the illustrations. Also I appreciate the help my daughter Susan gave with the illustrations.

Foreword

Children often identify with the feelings, thoughts and actions of characters in stories, whether or not the stories are fictional or true. This adventure of two fictional children who interact with the true story of Jesus and His Disciples gives insights which will likely prompt many questions from the reader or listener.

While some primary children would be able to read these accounts for themselves, the stories would be a good resource for reading to groups of children or perhaps be a before bedtime read when often real, heartfelt questions are asked.

One thing is sure. The children here meet Jesus with their feelings, experience and wonder. That is indeed good.

Vicki Shaver
Worked with Scripture Union before becoming the Lecturer in Children's Ministry at the International Christian College

Story 1 - The First Christmas

Chapter One – A Special Baby is Born

(Matthew 1 & Luke 1:26-38, 2:1-20.)

Long, long ago, in a country far away, there lived a little girl whose name was Sarah. Sarah and her brother Reuben lived in a small town called Bethlehem with their mother Joanne and father Simon. Simon's job was to take care of any travellers who arrived at their house looking for a place to stay. Sarah and Reuben often helped their parents to look after the travellers.

One day Bethlehem was especially busy. Lots of travellers were looking for a place to stay. Many people were staying at Sarah's house.

"Sarah, Reuben, will you run to the well and get me some more water?" their mother asked, handing them a pot each. "There are so many people arriving today that I need more water for them to wash their feet."

Sarah and Reuben hurried to the well in the middle of the village. As they went along the street Sarah noticed that there were lots of people queuing up in front of a table. Two Roman soldiers, with large bronze helmets, were guarding the table.

"Where have all these people come from?" asked Sarah. "It's not usually as busy as this."

"It has something to do with a census," explained Reuben as they pushed their way through the crowds.

"What's a census?" asked Sarah.

"Father tried to explain it to me," said Reuben. "It has something to do with being counted. Everyone has to go back to the town where they were born. All these people, who have come to Bethlehem, must have been born here."

"Who's going to count them all?" asked Sarah as they arrived at the well.

"I don't know," replied Reuben.

There were lots of people at the well. As they waited their turn to get water, Sarah noticed their friend James.

"Shalom James, do you need water too?" she called out to him.

"Shalom Sarah. Shalom Reuben," said James coming over to meet his friends. "Yes, we need more water as we have relatives staying with us. My dad says there's no room for anyone else in Bethlehem tonight."

"I know," said Reuben, "we are full too. Some travellers will have to sleep outside on the roof."

When it was their turn, they filled the pots with water and placed them on their heads. The sun was setting as they made their way home.

People were coming and going everywhere. A Roman centurion rode up the narrow street on a beautiful black horse. Donkeys plodded slowly along carrying heavy bundles on their backs. Camels walked carefully through the crowds. A troop of noisy soldiers marched quickly past them. Children ran about excitedly as they had never seen their village so busy with all the strangers. Sarah, Reuben and James stood and watched all that was going on before they went home.

"What took you so long?" asked Joanne as the children came in the door.

"Everyone was at the well tonight," said Sarah pouring some water from her pot into two large bowls. "We met James there. They have people staying with them too."

Sarah took the bowls of water to the travellers so that they could wash their feet.

Reuben took his water jar to the stable and filled the trough for the animals to drink. He made sure the horses and donkeys had plenty of straw to lie down on. Then he brought some hay to feed the animals.

As Reuben left the stable he looked up at the bright stars sparkling in the dark sky. He hoped everyone had found a place to stay for the night.

Just as he was about to go into his house Reuben noticed a man leading a donkey coming slowly towards him. A woman was sitting on the donkey.

The man called out to Reuben, "Excuse me; have you any room in your house tonight?"

"I'm sorry," replied Reuben, "there is no room here or anywhere else in Bethlehem. You are too late. Every house is full of people."

The man and the donkey stopped right beside the house. Reuben looked at the woman sitting uncomfortably on the donkey's back. She looked exhausted.

"We've been travelling for five days now and we are very tired. My wife is about to have her baby," he said anxiously, "Can you help us please?"

Reuben felt sorry for the couple but he knew there was no room anywhere. He wondered what he could do.

"Wait here," he said hurriedly. "I will ask my mother to come and help you. You can't stay in the house as there are people everywhere, but I have an idea."

Reuben rushed into the house shouting, "Mother, Mother, there's a poor couple outside needing a place to stay. The lady is about to have her baby. They are very tired as they have been travelling for five days."

"Where can we put a lady who is about to have a baby?" said Joanne sadly, "there is no room anywhere."

"I know, but what about the cave at the back of our house where the cow is?" suggested Reuben excitedly, "it's warm and quiet in there. I can put some fresh straw down on the floor for her to rest on."

"Oh, please let her stay," pleaded Sarah who wanted to see the new baby when it was born. "I'll fetch some water for her. We must have some food left over for them."

"Well, she certainly can't have her baby here," said Joanne. "Reuben, take them to the cave. Sarah, get the water. I will find some strips of linen cloth to wrap the baby in. Your father will have to attend to the travellers here," she added as she rushed off.

Reuben ran outside again and took hold of the donkey.

"Follow me," he said leading the donkey round the back of the house. He stopped at the stable to get some fresh straw and some hay for the donkey. Then he took them to a small cave near the house. The man lifted the woman off the donkey and they followed Reuben into the cave. By the light of the moon they could just make out the walls.

"You can stay in here," said Reuben laying the straw on the floor at the back of the cave. "It's quiet and warm and no one will disturb you. My mother will bring a couple of lamps and some things for you. Sarah, my sister, is getting you warm water. Is there anything else you need? Oh, my name is Reuben."

"Thank you, Reuben," said the man, "My name is Joseph and this is my wife Mary." Joseph helped Mary sit down on the fresh clean straw.

Reuben filled the cow's feeding trough with new hay and scattered some on the ground for the donkey to eat.

"Thank you so much for helping us," said Mary softly. She tried to settle herself on the straw, rubbing her back.

Reuben brought the donkey into the cave and tied it to a post beside their cow. He then hurried off to get them some food. Joseph unloaded their belongings from the donkey and gave it a pat. Just then Joanne arrived carrying a couple of lamps and a blanket and some bits of cloth.

"Shalom, I am Joanne. How are you feeling?" she asked putting down the bundle. "You can cover the straw with this blanket. It will be more comfortable to lie on. We have a little food left over but it has been a busy day here. I had to bake bread three times today. Ah, here comes Sarah with some water."

Sarah put the bowl on the floor beside Mary and handed her a small towel.

"Thank you Sarah," she said as she began to wash her hands and face. Sarah knelt down beside Mary and washed her feet.

"That is kind of you," said Mary, "I can't reach my feet these days. Once the baby comes I will be able to wash my own feet again," she added with a laugh.

"Is the baby coming soon?" asked Sarah, looking up and taking the towel from Mary. Sarah carefully dried Mary's feet with the towel.

"Babies come when they are ready," said Joanne, trying to make Mary as comfortable as possible.

Reuben arrived with a basket of bread and some fruit which he handed to Joseph.

"Now off you two go," instructed their mother. "I will stay with Mary for a while. Tell your father I'm out here helping Mary."

Sarah wanted to stay and see if the baby was coming that night but she knew her mother wouldn't let her.

"I don't think I will sleep tonight," Sarah told Reuben as they went into the house. "It's so exciting to have a baby born here. Do you think it will come tonight?"

"Maybe," replied Reuben, "I think that is why Mother is staying with Mary. She didn't want us there."

"I wonder if it will be a boy or a girl," said Sarah.

"Where have you two been and where is your mother?" asked their father as he rolled out two mats and laid them on the floor. "You should be asleep by now; lie down on the mats. We will have to sleep here near the door as there is no room anywhere else."

"The couple who arrived late tonight are in the cave beside our cow," explained Reuben proudly. "It was my idea that they could go there. I think she might be having her baby soon."

"And Mother is with her," whispered Sarah, "Her name is Mary. Do you think the baby will come tonight?"

"I don't know," replied their father quietly, "but it was a good idea Reuben to put them in the cave. She certainly couldn't have had her baby here. I hope she is all right. The cave is not the best place to have a baby but then it is better than outside in the fields."

Simon rolled out another two mats laying them on the floor next to the children. He brought some blankets and gave one to each of them.

"Now go to sleep you two, it's very late and we will have to be up early to feed all these travellers before they leave."

"I can't get to sleep," said Sarah, "I am too excited about the baby."

"Shh!" said her father sleepily.

Sarah tried to close her eyes but she was too wide awake. She lay quietly listening to all the noises in the room. People were snoring, someone turned over muttering something in their sleep but there was no sound of a baby crying.

Just then Joanne came hurrying into the house carrying a light. She went to the big box at the back of the room and took out some clean cloth.

"Is the baby coming tonight?" whispered Sarah.

"I thought you were asleep," replied her mother reaching up to the shelf to get a large jar. "Yes, the baby will be born tonight. I forgot to take the salt with me and I need more fresh cloths to wrap the baby in."

"What do you need salt for?" asked Sarah quietly.

"After a baby is born you need to wash it and rub salt over the body to prevent any infection," whispered Joanne as she hurried out the door. "Go to sleep now. You will see the baby in the morning."

After her mother had left the house Sarah whispered, "Are you asleep Reuben?"

"No, I can't sleep. There is too much going on." replied Reuben softly, not wanting to wake their father.

The children lay quietly on their mats waiting for their mother to return with news about the birth of the baby.

"It's taking a long time," said Sarah after a while. She sat up and looked about the dark room. Suddenly the room was lit up by a bright light shining through the small window at the back of the house. Reuben got up, carefully climbed over the sleeping travellers and went over to the big box by the wall. He stood on it to look out of the window.

"Look Sarah," he exclaimed, "The sky is all lit up. It's as if there is a bright light in the sky!"

Sarah jumped up and quietly went to where Reuben was standing.

"Let me see, let me see," she whispered trying to climb onto the big box. Reuben lifted her up so that she could look out of the small window.

"Wow, the whole sky is on fire," she exclaimed quietly.

Reuben put her down, and they carefully made their way back to their mats.

"I want to see that amazing sky," whispered Reuben quietly watching the bright light shining through the small window.

"Oh! The light has gone!" said Sarah sadly after a while when she realised the room was in darkness once more. Before Reuben could answer, their mother returned. Quickly they lay down pretending to be asleep.

"It's a boy," whispered Joanne to her husband as she lay down beside him.

"Is everything all right?" grunted Simon still half asleep.

"Mother and baby are both doing fine," she replied with a yawn.

The children waited till they were sure their mother and father were asleep. Then Sarah tapped Reuben on his shoulder.

"Let's go and see the baby," she whispered.

Reuben stood up and helped Sarah to her feet. As their eyes got used to the darkness, they carefully made their way to the door. Neither said a word till they were safely outside.

"Look, the sky is dark just like it always is," said Reuben disappointedly as he looked up. "I wonder what made it so bright."

The children crept quietly round the back of the house to the cave.

"What if Mary is sleeping?" said Sarah in a quiet voice.

"Look, there's a light in the cave" said Reuben, "we can go and see if they are awake."

Sarah and Reuben crept into the cave and saw Mary cradling the baby in her arms.

"We couldn't sleep," said Sarah quietly not wanting to wake the baby.

"Can we come in?" asked Reuben politely.

"Yes," said Mary, placing Jesus in the manger, "come and meet my little son Jesus."

"You have a name for the baby already!" said Reuben in surprise.

"Yes," said Joseph, "we were told to call Him Jesus."

"So you knew it was going to be a boy," said Sarah in amazement.

"I see you have used the cow's manger for a cradle," said Reuben looking about the cave.

"I made a beautiful cradle for Him," said Joseph. "It is at our home in

Nazareth. We couldn't bring it with us. The poor donkey had enough to carry."

"I'm sure our cow won't mind you borrowing her feeding trough," said Reuben. "There's fresh hay in it. If you put some of the cloths on top of the hay Jesus won't feel itchy or uncomfortable."

"You are a very thoughtful boy, Reuben," said Mary, lifting baby Jesus out of the manger to let Sarah put some cloth over the hay. "There, I think He likes His new cradle."

"It's probably not as nice as the one Joseph made for Him though," said Sarah pushing down the hay to make sure there were no bits sticking out that might scratch baby Jesus. "But how did you know it was to be a boy?"

Before Joseph could answer there was a noise outside and four shepherds came running in. The shepherds knelt down in front of the baby.

"You won't believe this," panted one of the shepherds trying to get his breath back, "an angel came to us while we were watching our sheep up on the hillside. He told us not to be afraid, that he had come to tell us about a great and joyful event which would be Good News for everyone!"

"Then the angel said that a Saviour had just been born in David's town, and we all know that Bethlehem is David's town," interrupted another shepherd excitedly, "This baby must be Christ the Lord!"

"The angel told us that we would find the baby wrapped in cloths and lying in a manger," continued the first shepherd.

"Then suddenly the whole sky was full of light and..."

"And there were lots of angels singing and praising God," added the fourth shepherd just as excited as the others.

"So we decided to see this wonderful event for ourselves," said the fourth shepherd. "We started looking for a place where there would be a manger."

"When we saw the light shining from this cave we thought that this might be the place, so we came right in," one of the shepherds continued.

"Imagine God telling **us** about this special baby," said the first shepherd looking at Jesus. "Isn't it amazing that an angel would speak to ordinary simple shepherds?" he added.

"No one will believe we saw angels," said the young boy.

"We believe you," said Sarah quickly, "we saw the sky lit up, but we didn't hear any singing. That must have been awesome."

"Yes, we saw the bright light in the sky shining through our window," said Reuben. "Were you not afraid?"

"We were terrified," said the shepherds. "We covered our eyes and fell to the ground."

"I nearly ran away," said one of the shepherds.

"This is amazing," said Joseph. "Before you came in, I was just about to tell Reuben and Sarah about the angel who visited us."

"An angel visited you too!" said Sarah in surprise. "Tell us about the angel, please."

Everyone sat down on the ground and Joseph began to tell them about the amazing things that had happened.

"Mary, you begin," said Joseph.

"Well, one day, before I was married to Joseph," Mary began, "I was at home grinding some corn when suddenly an angel came into the courtyard. I saw the angel standing right in front of me. I was terrified just like you shepherds were. But the angel told me not to be afraid. He said God was pleased with me and that I was going to have a special baby. The angel told me I would give birth to a son and I was to name Him Jesus. He said Jesus would also be called the Son of God!"

"Wow!" said Sarah excitedly.

"Later an angel appeared to me too in a dream," continued Joseph. "He told me to marry Mary and not to be upset that Mary was pregnant. God's Holy Spirit had given her this special baby. Then the angel told me that Mary would have a son and that I was to name Him Jesus as He would save His people from their sins."

"So you took Mary home to be your wife," said Sarah triumphantly.

"Yes," said Joseph, "when I woke up I did what the angel told me to do. So here we are with baby Jesus just as the angel said."

"God sent angels to the shepherds too," said Sarah in amazement.

"And all this happened in our cave," Reuben said proudly.

"This is all very strange," said one of the shepherds getting to his feet. "We must go now as we need to get back to our sheep."

"I can't wait to tell everyone what happened tonight," said another of the shepherds.

"Everyone will be astonished when we tell them that angels told us about the birth of this special baby!" he added.

"They won't believe that we saw angels and heard them singing," said the young boy.

After they had gone, Mary leant against the wall of the cave and shut her eyes.

"What a night it has been. I will never forget all this," said Mary quietly to Joseph.

"Yes, we have experienced something wonderful tonight. This is certainly from God. Now try to sleep Mary, you have had a very tiring time," said Joseph, "I will watch over Jesus while you sleep."

Sarah and Reuben said goodnight to the little family and went out of the cave.

"I can't wait to tell our friend James," whispered Sarah excitedly as they crept quietly into the house.

The next day Joanne and Simon were busy attending to the travellers. Reuben was helping too, so Sarah went to see James to tell him the exciting news.

"You'll never believe what happened in our cave last night," began Sarah excitedly as she told James and his mother Rhoda about the birth of the special baby, the angels and the shepherds.

"The baby's name is Jesus and His mother is called Mary," said Sarah when she had finished telling them everything.

"Where are they going to stay?" asked Rhoda, "They can't travel home yet with a new-born baby. Your house is always busy so I don't think there will be room for them even after the travellers have gone. Are they still in your cave?"

"Yes," replied Sarah. "Our house is full of people and we think it will be busy for some time."

"They could stay with us," suggested James.

"I think that is a good idea, James. God would want us to help them," said Rhoda. "Sarah, tell your mother that the young couple can come and stay here.

Our relatives are leaving today. I will go and prepare a room for them now and we will come for them later today."

Just before sunset James and his mother arrived at the cave.

"Shalom," said Rhoda bowing to the little family. "My name is Mary too but I am known as Rhoda, and this is my son James. You are very welcome to stay at our house. We have plenty of room. Perhaps my husband Alphaeus can help you get some work later on."

"Thank you, Rhoda. That is very kind of you," said Joseph. "Mary won't be able to travel for some time yet, so we need a place to stay till we can go back to Nazareth."

James hurried into the house to tell Sarah and her mother the plan for Mary, Joseph and the baby to stay at their house. Sarah and Reuben went with James to the cave.

Joseph was lifting Jesus out of the manger as they came in. He handed the baby to Mary. "I am a carpenter and I can make all kinds of things, like a yoke for an ox or a plough for the farmer or furniture for the home," he told Rhoda.

"Thank you, Rhoda," said Mary. "We are ready to come with you. We don't have much with us but Joanne has given me some clothes. Will you take our donkey over to your house, James? I think I can manage a short walk."

"You'd better give the manger back to your cow, Reuben," said Joseph removing the cloth from the hay.

Reuben lifted the manger and took it to where the cow was standing looking about her.

"I'm sure our cow didn't mind lending her feeding trough to Jesus," said Reuben with a laugh. "I'll bring her some fresh hay."

He untied the donkey and led it outside. He handed the reins to James then went to the stable for some hay.

Just then Joanne came into the cave carrying some raisin cakes, fruit and tea.

"Let's all have something to eat before you go. I'm happy that everything has turned out so well," said Joanne. "Now we have new friends, Mary and Joseph."

"And don't forget Jesus," smiled Sarah. "He is our friend too."

Chapter Two - The Visit to Jerusalem

(Luke 2:21-38)

Mary and Joseph stayed at James' house. After forty days they took Jesus to Jerusalem to dedicate Him to God as was the custom. Sarah wanted to hear all about what happened in Jerusalem so she went to the road which led to Jerusalem to watch for Mary and Joseph coming back. Sarah had never been to the city.

After some time James arrived as he too wanted to hear all about the trip to Jerusalem. They waited excitedly for Joseph to return. Soon they noticed dust rising into the air in the distance.

"Look, that might be them coming now," Sarah exclaimed as she began to run down the road.

"Wait," shouted James, "it could be any traveller coming this way."

Sarah didn't wait. She was sure it was Mary's donkey that was kicking up all the dust. Waving her hands in the air, she ran along the dry dirt road. James watched the travellers coming nearer. He saw Sarah stop and talk to them. Then he saw them all walking together.

"It must be Joseph," James said out loud.

"Shalom," shouted Joseph as they came nearer. James ran to meet them.

"What was it like in Jerusalem?" he asked excitedly. "What was the Temple like, Joseph? Did anything happen when you were there?"

"I'll walk for a little bit," said Mary handing Jesus to Sarah. "I'm a bit stiff and sore from sitting on the donkey." Joseph helped Mary get down from the donkey.

"Do you want a ride home Sarah?" asked Joseph when Mary took the baby from Sarah.

"Oh yes please, Joseph," answered Sarah happily.

Joseph gave the reins to James, then helped Sarah up onto the donkey's back.

"James, you can lead the donkey and Sarah can ride home," said Joseph.

"We have lots to tell you," said Mary, "But let's wait till we get home. I'm sure Rhoda wants to hear all about it too."

When they arrived at Rhoda's house she brought food and something to drink. Everyone gathered round anxious to hear all about their trip to Jerusalem. Alphaeus joined the others as he wanted to hear all about it too.

"We arrived in Jerusalem about noon, and went through the Golden Gate," Joseph began. "We started to climb the steps into the Temple. The Temple is very big, James, with large marble pillars. Then we went through to the Court of the Gentiles. It was very busy and noisy there. The courtyard was full of priests, musicians and worshippers. There were many stalls where traders were selling birds and animals for sacrifice. We tied the donkey to a post and bought a pair of doves. This is what we have to do according to our Law. The Law of Moses says that every first born son has to be dedicated to God."

"Then we made our way to the Court of the Women," continued Mary. "Just as we were taking the pair of doves to one of the Priests, an old man suddenly walked towards us. He came up to us and took Jesus in his arms."

"His name is Simeon," continued Joseph, "and God had told him that he wouldn't die before he had seen the Messiah, the Son of God."

"Simeon praised God and said some wonderful things about Jesus and His future," said Mary excitedly. "We were speechless with surprise at what he said."

"We know Jesus is a special baby," said Sarah, "but how did Simeon know?"

"God must have told him that Jesus was the one he had been waiting for," said Joseph.

"That's amazing. Imagine an old man in Jerusalem knowing about Jesus," said Sarah.

"That's not all Sarah," said Joseph. "As Simeon was praying for Jesus, an old lady came over. Her name is Anna and she is a prophetess. She is very old and lives in the Temple worshipping God every day. She too knew that Jesus is special."

"Anna began praising God and telling everyone in the Temple that Jesus is the one they have been prayerfully expecting," said Mary lifting Jesus up in the air and kissing Him.

"Wow," said James in amazement.

As they listened, Rhoda and Alphaeus were surprised at what they heard.

When everyone had finished eating, Sarah went home. She couldn't wait to tell Reuben and her mother and father all about Simeon and Anna. They too were amazed when they heard about the two people at the Temple who recognised that Jesus was special. Joanne praised God for sending Jesus into the world.

Story 2 - The Wise Men

Chapter One - Strange Visitors

(Matthew 2:1-18)

Simon and Joanne's home was the first house in Bethlehem. They shared their home with any traveller who needed a place to stay. Their children, Reuben and Sarah, liked it when travellers stayed with them. One evening Sarah was on the roof of their house helping her mother gather up the washing that was drying on the wall that surrounded the roof.

"Reuben, come quickly, camels are coming along the road," Sarah shouted to her brother who was busy in the courtyard below. Reuben ran quickly up the narrow stairs to the flat roof and looked over the wall towards the road.

"You're right; camels are coming along the road. Look Mother," said Reuben pointing to the group of travellers. Joanne put down her basket of washing and came over to where the children were.

"Well, I wonder where they are heading," said Joanne. "We don't often see men, dressed like that, coming here. You'd better call your father, Reuben; they may want to stay here for the night."

Reuben and Sarah ran down the stairs. Reuben went to look for his father while Sarah went along the road to meet the strange travellers.

"Do you want to stay at our house?" Sarah asked them. "We have plenty of room. Our house is just over there," she added pointing to her house.

The strangers reined in their camels and one of them made his camel kneel on the road. He climbed down from his camel and looked at Sarah. Sarah noticed his colourful cloak and unusual turban that he wore on his head. She had never seen such strangers before and wondered who they were.

Just then Reuben arrived with his father.

"Shalom! You are most welcome to stay the night in our home," said Simon bowing to the stranger standing beside his camel.

The stranger bowed to Simon and said, "We study the stars and many months ago we discovered a bright new star in the Eastern sky. We looked up our scrolls. In one of them it was written that when this particular star appeared it was a sign that a king had been born. We are looking for this king."

"Are you Wise Men then?" asked Sarah who always wanted to know everything.

"You could call us that I suppose," laughed another of the men making his camel kneel down. "We are astrologers and the star led us to Jerusalem."

Simon said nothing as he watched the rest of the strangers make their camels kneel down so that they could dismount.

"King Herod was as surprised as we were when the Jewish teachers told him that the baby would be born in Bethlehem," said the first Wise Man loosening the strap round the camel's middle. "We have come to Bethlehem to worship this new-born king."

"You spoke to King Herod!" said Reuben in surprise.

"Well, you would expect a king to be born in a palace wouldn't you?" he replied. "Not in some small unimportant town like Bethlehem."

"They must be looking for Jesus," whispered Sarah to her father.

"A baby was born here some time ago," said Simon realising that it was Jesus they were looking for. He didn't know what to say, as he wasn't sure if he should tell them where Jesus and His family were living now.

"You can rest here for the night," said Simon. "My son will help you unload the camels. Sarah, fetch some water for our visitors and tell your mother to prepare a meal."

"Thank you," said the first Wise Man. "We will stay with you tonight then continue our search in the morning."

The first Wise Man opened a large bag which was strapped onto his camel's saddle. He took out a gold box and examined it carefully. Another two men took packages out of their bags. Then the three Wise Men followed Sarah into the house. The other members of the group began to remove the saddles from the camels and unload their belongings. Then they made the camels get up and handed the reins to Simon who led then all into the stable. Reuben helped to carry the saddles into the stable. The saddles had a strong smell of camels.

When they had settled in, Joanne served them some food. Sarah and Reuben watched them carefully, wondering what was in the three packages.

"Do you think there is gold inside that box?" whispered Reuben to Sarah.

"It must be something precious as he has not let it out of his sight all evening," replied Sarah. "They must have brought gifts for the king they are looking for."

When the men had finished their meal they all went outside. Three of them were still carrying their gifts. Thinking they were going to check on their camels Sarah and Reuben followed them. They hid behind the wall of their house so that the men wouldn't see them.

They saw one of the Wise Man looking up into the dark sky.

They heard him say, "See, there is our bright star."

The children watched as the men talked together trying to decide what to do. Then some of the men went into the stable to feed the camels, but the three men, who were carrying the gifts, began to walk down the road. They kept looking and pointing to the sky as they went. Sarah and Reuben decided to follow them. As they walked slowly behind the men, Reuben wondered if the star would lead them to James' house. Sarah hoped that the Wise Men wouldn't realise they were following them. The street was busy with people buying and selling. When they saw the strangers passing by they stopped what they were doing and looked at them. It was most unusual to see such important visitors in their town. Sarah felt afraid yet excited.

"It will be amazing if the star does lead them to James' house," Sarah whispered.

Suddenly the three Wise Men stopped. "Look, the star is right above this house," said one of them staring up at the sky.

Sarah and Reuben looked up too. They could not believe that the bright star was shining right above where they were.

"At last we have found our King," announced the first Wise Man.

"I'm overjoyed at finally finding this place," said another. "We have travelled such a long way. It has taken us many months. Now at last we are here."

Just then Sarah noticed James standing at the door of his house staring at the strange men in amazement. They heard one Wise Man say, "We have come to worship the new King."

James left the three Wise Men standing at the door and ran to get Joseph who was in the courtyard feeding the donkey. Sarah and Reuben heard James calling Joseph.

"We should go back home," said Reuben quietly.

"I want to stay and see what they have brought for Jesus," said Sarah.

"No, we had better go home and tell Father what has happened. We certainly didn't expect the star to lead them right to where Jesus is," said Reuben walking back down the road. "Come on Sarah, James will tell us all about it in the morning."

The children walked slowly home thinking about how the star had led the three Wise Men to the exact place they were looking for.

When their father heard about it he said, "This must be from God. Only God would send these men to worship Jesus. Don't worry, everything will be all right. Now off to bed you two."

"But these strangers aren't Jews like us, Father, are they?" asked Sarah. "Do they worship our God?"

"Would our God speak to Gentiles?" Reuben asked.

"You children ask too many questions," said their mother laying their mats on the floor. "It's time for you to go to sleep."

"That is a good question, Reuben," replied his father. "I don't know the answer but if God wants to speak to people from other nations, then I think He will."

Later that night when everyone was asleep Sarah was awakened by a strange noise. She woke Reuben and asked him if he had heard anything. He sat up sleepily and listened.

"You're right," whispered Reuben after some time. "I can hear voices. Perhaps someone is in the stable."

"Let's go and see," said Sarah standing up and walking quietly towards the door. Reuben followed trying not to make a sound.

When they were outside the house they noticed one of the Wise Men walking over to the stable carrying his bedding roll.

"What's he doing with his bedding roll at this time of the night?" whispered Sarah.

"Perhaps he is going to sleep with the camels," replied Reuben.

As they watched, they saw him lead one of the camels out of the stable.

He tied his camel to a post then went back into the stable.

"He's not going to sleep, I think he's leaving!" said Reuben in surprise.

"Why would he leave in the middle of the night without telling anyone?" asked Sarah almost in tears. "I think something is wrong."

"So do I," whispered Reuben not wanting anyone to hear him.

"Let's go and ask him," suggested Sarah who always wanted to know what was going on.

"I don't think we should," said Reuben stopping Sarah going over to the stable.

"Yes, we must find out why they are leaving," said Sarah pulling away from Reuben's grip. Sarah began to walk over to the stable.

"Wait for me," said Reuben hurrying to catch up with his sister.

They went into the stable where two of the Wise Men were putting the saddles onto their camels.

"Why are you leaving?" Sarah asked.

"What!" exclaimed the man in surprise. "What are you doing out here in the middle of the night? You gave me such a fright coming into the stable like that."

"I'm sorry," said Sarah, "I didn't mean to frighten you. We saw one of the camels outside the stable and wondered if you were leaving."

"God has spoken to us in a frightening dream," began the first Wise Man.

"We all woke up suddenly and just knew this was a warning from an angel of the Lord. We have to leave right away," said the second Wise

Man throwing his big bag over his saddle. "We think we are in danger from King Herod, and so is Jesus."

"We are not going back to King Herod to tell him where the King of the Jews is," said the first Wise Man. "We are going back to our country by a different route."

"But we must hurry," said the other Wise Man leading his camel out of the stable. "I've woken the others. King Herod will be waiting for us to return to him. When we don't show up he'll probably send his soldiers to look for us."

The other men came hurrying into the stable carrying their bedding rolls. They tied their belongings onto their camels and tightened the straps of their saddles. They too wondered why they were leaving in the middle of the night.

"Oh, this is awful," said Sarah. "We need to warn Mary and Joseph. Do you think King Herod isn't pleased to hear about another king in his land?"

"Yes, I think you should warn Joseph," said the first Wise Man. "It's not safe for them to stay in Bethlehem. King Herod knows the child was to be born here. I don't think he will want another king in Judea."

"Come on," shouted Sarah running out of the stable, "we must go and tell Mary and Joseph."

"But they will be asleep," said Reuben running after Sarah. "Maybe we should wait till the morning."

"It might be too late by the morning," said Sarah who was thinking about Herod and what he might do to Jesus. She was also worried about the Wise Men's frightening dream.

Sarah and Reuben hurried to James' house. As they came near they noticed a light shining out from the open door. Then they saw Joseph leading the donkey towards the house.

"Why have you brought the donkey to the house, Joseph?" asked Reuben.

"What are you two doing out here in the dark?" asked Joseph tying the donkey to a post.

"We came to warn you," said Sarah, "but why are you out here in the middle of the night?"

"We are leaving," said Joseph, "I was woken up by a strange dream. God told me to take Jesus away from here as it is no longer safe to stay in Bethlehem. Mary is getting everything ready. We must go tonight."

Just then Mary came out of the house carrying a sleepy Jesus.

"Can I help you?" asked Sarah, "I can hold Jesus for you if you want,"

"Oh, thank you Sarah," said Mary handing Jesus to her, "but what are you two doing here? You should be asleep in your own house."

"Reuben, tell Joseph about the Wise Men's dream," said Sarah rocking Jesus back to sleep.

Reuben told them about the Wise Men being woken by a frightening dream too and that they were leaving Bethlehem right away. He explained that the Wise Men didn't want anyone to see them go and that they were going back to their own country by another route.

When Joseph heard what Reuben said he was amazed yet worried.

"Have you got everything Mary? We have no time to waste," said Joseph hurrying back into the house. Mary followed him. Reuben stayed beside the donkey while Sarah walked up and down cuddling Jesus.

Soon Joseph returned and placed a large bundle of things over the donkey's back. Mary handed Joseph a large goatskin of water which he tied to the saddle. James' mother, Rhoda, came out carrying a cloth bag with some food in it. Joseph helped Mary onto the donkey and Sarah handed Jesus to His mother.

"I think Jesus has gone back to sleep," she whispered.

Rhoda handed the bag of food to Joseph, "Take this for the journey. It will be some time till you find a place to stop and rest."

"Thank you Rhoda," said Joseph tying it to the side of the saddle. "You have all been so kind to us. Thank you."

"Yes, I don't know what we would have done without your help. Thank you and God bless you all," cried Mary.

"Where are you going to go?" asked Sarah, tears streaming down her face.

"We are going to Egypt," said Joseph. "It will be safe there till God tells us when it's the right time to return home."

"Will you go back to Nazareth?" asked Reuben remembering that Mary and Joseph came from there.

"Yes, we will probably go back home eventually. I have my carpenter's business there," said Joseph untying the rope and giving the donkey a slap to make it move.

Sarah, Reuben and Rhoda watched the donkey walk slowly down the road with its precious load on its back.

"Do you think we will ever see them again?" said Sarah sadly, wiping her eyes.

Chapter Two – Leaving

Early next morning Simon came hurrying into the house shouting, "They've gone, vanished."

"Who's gone?" asked Joanne bringing some freshly baked bread into the room.

"The Wise Men have gone, all the men and their camels," said Simon.

Sarah and Reuben woke with all the noise. They sat up quickly.

"What's wrong Father?" asked Reuben.

"They've gone; the camels, the servants and the Wise Men have gone," said Simon again. Joanne began to roll up the sleeping mats.

"It's all right, we know all about it," said Reuben jumping to his feet wide awake now.

"What do you know all about?" asked his father shooing the hens out into the courtyard.

Reuben began to tell his parents all about what had happened. When he had finished he said, "Isn't God amazing, telling the Wise Men not to go back to King Herod?"

"And warning Joseph to take Mary and Jesus to safety in Egypt," added Sarah. "Do you think we will ever see them again?"

"It all seems strange to me," said Joanne comforting Sarah who was crying.

"And we knew nothing about it," said Simon in surprise.

"Do you think King Herod will come here?" Sarah asked between sobs. "Do you think they will kill us for looking after Jesus?"

"Don't be silly," said her father. "No one is going to kill anyone."

Just then James and his mother Rhoda came to their door.

"Did you see them go, Reuben?" asked James as they entered the room. "I wish I had woken up. I missed all the excitement last night."

The children were sent outside while Rhoda talked with Simon and Joanne.

Reuben told James all about what had happened during the night.

"Tell us about the gifts they gave to Jesus, James," asked Reuben when he had finished telling him about the escape in the middle of the night.

"Well," began James slowly, "When I saw these three strange men standing at our door, I ran to get Joseph who was in the courtyard feeding his donkey. I told him he would not believe who had come to see Jesus. Joseph was very surprised to see the colourfully dressed strangers at our door. He welcomed them and invited them into our house. Jesus was sitting on Mary's knee."

"Was Jesus scared when He saw them?" asked Sarah who wanted to know everything.

"No, He just looked at them and smiled," continued James. "The

Wise men knelt down in front of Jesus. Then one offered Him a beautiful golden box and opened the lid."

"What was in the box?" asked Reuben excitedly.

"Gold," replied James.

"Wow, Gold! I thought there would be gold in that box," said Reuben.

James continued, "Then Joseph came forward, thanked the Wise Man for his gift and placed the box on the ground beside Mary."

"What happened next?" Reuben asked.

"He went to the back of the room and stood watching the others give their gifts," James told them. "Then the second Wise Man offered his gift. It was a small leather pouch full of pieces of frankincense. I know because I saw him open the bag and pour some pieces onto his hand to show Mary."

"What's frankincense?" asked Sarah.

"It's a kind of gum taken from the Boswellia tree," explained James. "You can burn it and it makes a sweet smell. Priests use it in the Temple."

"How did you know that?" asked Reuben.

"I asked my dad after they had gone," replied James with a laugh. "They cut the bark of the tree and the resin seeps out. It's very expensive."

"What did the third Wise Man give Jesus?" asked Sarah.

"He had a beautiful golden jar. He told Mary it was full of myrrh. He said it was for later or something like that; I didn't understand what he said. He didn't open it."

"I know what myrrh is," said Reuben proudly. "It's a kind of perfume used to embalm a dead body. The resin from a tree can be made into an ointment."

"What would a baby want that for?" asked Sarah in surprise.

"I don't know but it too is very expensive," said James.

"They brought these special gifts for Jesus," said Reuben. "The Wise Men must be rich!"

"I wonder what my mother is telling your parents," said James after the children had been talking together for some time.

They decided to listen at the door. They heard Simon say, "Who said anything about soldiers? Danger, danger, soldiers, camels gone in the middle of the night. Things like that don't happen here. Bethlehem is a quiet town."

Then Sarah heard her mother speak.

"Rhoda may be right Simon. Just think, our house is near the road to Jerusalem. This would be the first place they would look."

"Looking for what?" she heard her father say.

Sarah couldn't stand it anymore and burst into the house.

"The soldiers will come looking for Jesus, Father," cried Sarah running to her mother.

"I'm afraid Sarah is right," said Rhoda quietly. "The Wise Men went to King Herod looking for the King of the Jews. The Jewish teachers told Herod that it was prophesised that the King would be born in Bethlehem. We all know that King Herod would not like another king in his land."

Simon suddenly understood the danger they were in. He stood up and put his arms round the boys.

"We have to leave here," he told them. "Reuben, James, run to the well and get some water for the journey. Don't talk to anyone. Don't tell anyone we are going away. And no, Sarah, before you ask, you can't go with them. You need to help your mother pack up some things. I'll get our donkey ready."

"What will you do Rhoda?" asked Joanne as she gathered up the sleeping mats.

"I think we are going to leave. I'm afraid. Alphaeus thinks we could be in danger too," said Rhoda. "James, you and Reuben get the water, then come back to our house. We will decide what to do and tell you what our plans are. Remember; don't tell anyone we are leaving."

James and Reuben went to the well. While they were getting the water, James told Reuben he had a secret.

"What secret?" asked Reuben, "You can tell me, I won't tell anyone else, I promise."

"I like your sister, Sarah," he blurted out.

"I know you do," said Reuben with a laugh. "Sarah likes you too!"

"But we won't be able to see each other now that you are leaving," said James sadly.

"Don't worry James, we'll think of something," said Reuben reassuringly. The boys walked slowly to James' house thinking of a way they could all meet up again.

Meanwhile Sarah and her mother packed up their belongings. By the time Reuben arrived back, Simon had taken their belongings to the stable so that no one would see him tying everything onto the donkey.

"It's just as well we have no travellers here today," said Joanne when her husband came into the house. "What are we going to do with our house? We have a good business here. We can't just leave it empty."

"I've thought about that," replied Simon. "Old Joshua down the road always wanted to buy an Inn for his son. I'll go and see him now. Perhaps he will buy it from us."

"But what will you tell him?" asked Reuben fearfully.

"Don't worry Reuben, I'll think of something," replied Simon. "What are Alphaeus' plans?"

"They're going to their uncle's house. He will look after them for a while till things settle down here," said Reuben handing the pot of water to his mother.

"Get the goatskin for me Reuben, so I can fill it," said Joanne pointing to the goatskin hanging on the wall under the shelf.

"When are we going?" asked Sarah who was now excited about this new adventure.

"We must wait till it is dark," said her father, "then we can slip out of the town and no one will know we have left. We will need to travel at night as far away from Jerusalem as possible. You children will need to try and rest now. We will eat before we leave."

"Where's Father going?" asked Sarah as she watched him go out of the door.

"He has gone to see old Joshua who might buy our house. We don't know when or if we will be back here," said her mother. "Now try and get some sleep. I will wake you when we are ready to leave."

"This is so exciting," said Sarah to Reuben as they went into one of the other rooms to rest. "I don't think I can sleep."

"I'm quite tired," yawned Reuben as he lay down on one of the mats. "After all we were up most of the night."

Before they knew it, they were both fast asleep.

Soon it was time to leave.

"I hope you had a good sleep," said their father as he came into the room. "We have a long journey ahead of us and you will have to walk. The donkey has enough to carry with all our belongings. Now wash your face and hands and come and have something to eat. We must leave in an hour."

"Will we be able to say goodbye to James?" asked Sarah suddenly realising they were going away for good.

"Yes, we will call in on our way out of the town. Hopefully no one will see us."

That night Sarah and Reuben sadly said goodbye to James before they left Bethlehem.

"We are trying to think up a way to meet up again soon," whispered James to Sarah as they said goodbye.

"Good," said Sarah with a smile. "I do hope we will see each other again."

James gave Reuben a knowing look. He didn't have a plan as yet but he knew that he would see Sarah and Reuben again one day soon.

Simon took his family to live near the River Jordan.

James and his family left the following day to visit their uncle.

Old Joshua bought Simon's house and the cow. He and his family moved into the Inn shortly afterwards.

Story 3 - A Special Occasion
Chapter One - A Surprise at Jerusalem
(Luke 2:41-52)

After the Wise Men had returned to their own country, Simon, Joanne and their children left Bethlehem too. They travelled to a small village near the River Jordan, where they found somewhere to live. Simon got a job there and the family soon settled in their new home. Alphaeus, Rhoda and James returned to Bethlehem after a few months. The two families had arranged to meet in Jerusalem each spring for the celebration of the Passover. They had agreed that every year they would meet up with each other at the crossroads going into Jerusalem. When Reuben and James were twelve years old they had gone to the Temple together for a special service of dedication to God.

Sarah is now twenty years old and Reuben and James are twenty two. It is spring, time to go to Jerusalem again for the Feast of the Passover. Everyone is getting ready for this special occasion.

"Is it time to go yet?" asked Sarah excitedly as she came through the door carrying her water pot.

"We're just waiting for Reuben," said her mother Joanne, holding the large goatskin for Sarah to fill with water.

"He always takes a long time getting ready when it is the Feast of the Passover," said Sarah a little annoyed at having to wait for him.

"Well, this Feast is very important to Reuben. He enjoys going with the men to the Temple and learning about God from the rabbis," explained her mother.

Joanne gathered together all the things she would need for the journey. She wrapped up her cooking pot, jars and utensils and put them into her basket. She then handed the basket to Sarah who carried it outside.

"Reuben, are you ready yet?" shouted Sarah as she stood waiting for her father to arrive with the donkey.

"I know why you are in such a hurry to go to Jerusalem," said Reuben as he came round from the back of the house. "You just can't wait to see James," teased Reuben with a laugh.

"Of course I want to see James," said Sarah feeling a little embarrassed. Everyone knew that James and Sarah loved each other and were going to be married soon.

"Joanne, have you got everything ready?" said Simon, as he led the old donkey up to the house. "We need to reach Jericho before the sun sets. We can stop there for the night."

Joanne and Sarah were waiting by the door. Sarah handed the basket to her father and he tied it carefully to the side of the donkey. Simon took the basket of food from Joanne and strapped it onto other side of the donkey.

"Sarah, you know that James and his family will be waiting for us at the crossroads going into Jerusalem," Joanne said, as she strapped the large goatskin of water onto the saddle. Joanne went back into the house to get the sleeping mats. She gave them to Simon who made sure they were tied tightly to the saddle. When he had made sure that nothing would fall off the donkey's back, the family set out on their journey to Jerusalem.

It took them two days to reach the outskirts of the city.

"Can you see James and Rhoda yet?" Sarah called out excitedly to Reuben who was leading the donkey.

"Not yet, Sarah," he answered, "but there are so many travellers making their way up to Jerusalem that I can't make out if James is there or not."

As they reached the crossroads, James and his family were sitting by the side of the road waiting for them. The two families greeted each other and exchanged their news. Alphaeus, Simon, and Reuben walked in front, while Joanne and Rhoda talked with each other as they walked along the road. Sarah and James followed behind them.

"Let's camp here," suggested Simon as they arrived among the olive trees on the Mount of Olives. "It's a bit quieter here than in the city."

"Good idea," said Alphaeus. "The women can prepare the evening meal while we go into Jerusalem."

The men helped to unload the donkeys before going to the Temple. Rhoda collected some stones, cleared a flat bit of ground and arranged the stones in a circle ready to make a fire. She then gathered some small sticks which she placed in the circle and lit the fire. Joanne prepared the vegetables, cutting up some cucumber, onions and leeks. She put them in a pot and placed the pot beside the fire. Sarah took some flour out of a linen bag and put it into a wooden bowl. Then she poured some water onto the flour, mixing the dough. She patted small bits of the bread mixture into circles. When the fire was hot enough, Rhoda put a large rock into the fire to heat it, ready to bake the unleavened bread.

"The men are taking a long time to return from the city," remarked Sarah as she placed one of the flat circles of dough on the hot rock to bake.

Just then Reuben and James came hurrying up to their camp site.

"You'll never guess who we've met," panted James excitedly. "Father is bringing them over right now."

"Who have you met?" asked Sarah.

"Jesus, we met Jesus up at the Temple!" said Reuben proudly. "Can you believe it, Sarah? Jesus is twelve years old now and Joseph has brought Him to the Temple for the Feast of the Passover."

"Oh, I can't wait to see Jesus," said Sarah in amazement. "How did you know it was Jesus, Reuben?"

"I recognised Mary and Joseph," he replied. "I was waiting at the entrance to the Temple when a crowd of worshippers passed by. Suddenly I saw Mary and Joseph with a young boy. I ran up to them and asked them if the boy was Jesus."

"Did they remember you?" asked Sarah.

"Only after I told them who I was," replied Reuben. "Look, here they come with Father."

There was great excitement when everyone met. Sarah couldn't wait to tell Jesus how she had looked after Him when He was a baby. Reuben wanted Jesus to know that it was his idea that Mary and Joseph used their cave because there was no room in their house. James explained to Jesus that it was his house they were living in when the Wise Men brought Him their gifts, and Mary told Joanne and Rhoda all about their time in Egypt.

"Joseph, have you a place to stay tonight?" asked Alphaeus.

"No, we had just arrived in Jerusalem when we met James," said Joseph. "We were so excited to see you that we came straight here."

"You can camp here with us," said Sarah quickly.

"Of course you must," added Joanne happily, "we have plenty of food and water to share with you."

"It will be like old times with us all together again," said Rhoda laughing.

"This is my first time in Jerusalem," said Jesus excitedly. "I can't wait to find out all about what goes on in the Temple."

The little group sat round the fire talking and eating. Simon explained to them that they had moved to another village near the River Jordan.

"I know that area," said Mary, "My cousin Elizabeth lives in the hill country of Judea near the River Jordan. Her husband, Zechariah, is a priest. I went to visit her before her baby, John, was born."

Sarah wanted to know everything about what happened after they left Bethlehem.

"Mary, how did you know when it was safe to leave Egypt?" she asked.

"Did God tell you in a dream again, Joseph?" wondered Reuben.

"Yes, Reuben," replied Joseph, "an angel came to me in a dream and told me it was safe to return to Israel. I was warned not to go to Judea, so we went back to Nazareth in Galilee. I have my carpenter business there and I'm showing Jesus how to carve wood."

"He is very good," said Mary proudly. "He carved me a beautiful bird for my birthday."

"Could Jesus come with us tomorrow to the Temple, Joseph?" asked Reuben.

"I would like to go with Reuben and James to the Temple," said Jesus looking at Joseph. "Would that be all right?"

Jesus was happy that He had met Reuben, Sarah and James.

"Yes, we can all go together," replied Joseph.

"We know some of the rabbis there. We can introduce you to them," said James.

It was late by the time everyone was asleep after the excitement of the day.

Chapter Two - The Feast of the Passover

(Exodus 12:1-28)

The next day all the men went to Jerusalem together. On the way they bought a year-old lamb from a merchant and took it to the Temple. The women prepared some food before they set off for Jerusalem. On the way Joanne told Mary that they were all excited and happy that Sarah and James were getting married soon.

"Oh, I am so pleased," said Mary as they walked through a crowded street. "I thought you both looked happy," she added smiling at Sarah.

"Sarah and I are looking for some material for a new dress," Joanne explained as they pushed past all the people thronging the market place. When they found the street which sold material Sarah and her mother went shopping while Rhoda and Mary walked up to the Temple. They arranged to meet later in the Court of the Women.

It was hot and the climb up to the Temple was steep. Rhoda stopped to get her breath back. As they rested Mary told Rhoda how happy she felt meeting up again with her old friends, who had been so helpful when they lived in Bethlehem.

At last they arrived at the Temple and went into the Court of the

Women. People were buying various animals and doves for the sacrifice. It was very busy and noisy. Sheep were bleating and the stall holders were shouting to the people to come and buy their goods. The women sat watching everything that was going on. When they heard the three blasts on the ram's horn they knew that the Passover sacrifice had begun.

"It's very hot and noisy with all the pilgrims and animals here," said Mary wiping her face.

"And a bit smelly too," added Rhoda fanning her face with the edge of her long veil. "I don't like the smell of blood, incense and burning fat."

A short time later Joanne and Sarah found them in the Court of the Women. They prayed together before the men returned from the ceremony.

"This is a very special occasion," said Mary wiping tears from her eyes.

"Yes Mary, we felt so proud of James and Reuben when they became an adult at our special Jewish ceremony," said Joanne.

"I am happy that Jesus has dedicated Himself to God today," said Mary. "He is very special and I am sure God has a great work for Him to do."

"We know Jesus is special, don't we Mother?" replied Sarah with a smile. "I love God and want to follow our Laws just as the men do. I wish women could go into the Inner Temple Court," she added thoughtfully.

"God knows how we feel and what is in our hearts," said Mary quietly.

The men arrived with the lamb and they all made their way back to the camp site struggling through the crowded streets. People were pushing their way between camels, horses and donkeys. A troop of soldiers marched past.

This reminded Rhoda of the soldiers who came to Bethlehem. Mary stopped when she saw them march past. "Did the soldiers come to Bethlehem after we left?" she asked quietly.

"Yes, so it was just as well you escaped," Rhoda answered.

"It must have been awful. Did many families suffer?" asked Mary.

"One or two did," Rhoda replied sadly.

"That all seems such a long time ago," said Mary with a sigh. "But it's something I'll never forget."

"We were afraid that the soldiers might come to our house," said Joanne sadly. "That's why we left Bethlehem too. We like living in the hill country now. Simon got work there and the children settled after a time."

"Although we missed James," added Sarah with a smile.

"When Sarah and James get married they will live with us," said Joanne. "Simon is getting old and suffers from back pain. James will be a great help to us."

The women filled their goatskins with water at a well before returning to the camp site to prepare the lamb for the special meal. Before the lamb was cooked Joseph dipped a hyssop branch in the blood from the lamb just as Moses would have done over a thousand years before. Then Joanne used a branch from the pomegranate tree as a spit to roast the lamb over the fire. At this meal they ate unleavened bread and bitter herbs. Everyone enjoyed this special meal together. At the end of the meal, as Jesus was the youngest male, it was His turn to ask the questions.

"Why is this night different from any other night and why do we eat unleavened bread?" asked Jesus.

"This is the night we remember when God rescued the Israelites from Egypt where they were slaves," Joseph answered. "We eat unleavened bread to remind us that the Israelites had to escape in a hurry, so they didn't have time to wait for the bread to rise. They just brought their dough without adding any yeast."

"Why did we roast the lamb and only have bitter herbs?" was the next questions Jesus had to ask.

"The bitter herbs we ate tonight helps us to think about the hard times our ancestors had in Egypt and the lamb was roasted just as they did the night they escaped from Egypt."

The final question asked was why they dipped their bread in salt water. Joseph explained that the salty water represented the tears their forefathers shed because they were slaves.

"Why did you dip the branch into the lamb's blood?" asked Reuben who wanted to be reminded about this part of the ritual.

"God told the Israelites to put the blood on their door posts so that every house that had this sign was safe from the angel of death. That is why we call this feast Passover," answered Simon.

"I don't like that bit about the angel of death but I'm glad death passed over our ancestors," said Sarah.

"This was the only way Pharaoh would let the slaves leave," James reminded her. "When all the first born Egyptians died, Pharaoh let God's people go."

"I know, but I still don't like that part of the story," said Sarah.

"Now we need to pray to God to deliver us from the oppressive rule of the Romans," said Simon.

"You are an adult now, Jesus, so You can come with us tomorrow into the inner courtyard and listen to the Teachers of the Law," said Joseph.

"That will be wonderful," replied Jesus. "I want to know all about our Jewish religion."

They stayed in Jerusalem for several days enjoying being together again and going to the Temple to worship. When it was time to leave, Joseph, Alphaeus and Simon helped load up the donkeys. They decided to travel together for the first part of the journey. When everything was ready Mary asked, "Has anyone seen Jesus?"

"He will still be at the Temple with James and Reuben," said Rhoda smiling. "But don't worry Mary, they will be along soon. James is always last to leave the Temple."

"He asks too many questions," added Sarah with a laugh.

"We'll wait for them at the crossroads," said Simon. "It's too crowded here, better to get out onto the open road and wait there."

"That's what we usually do," said Alphaeus pulling the donkey. "If anyone gets separated in the crowd we have arranged to meet up at the crossroads."

The women walked together, talking about the wedding while Alphaeus, Simon and Joseph led their heavily-laden donkeys along the dusty road.

Chapter Three – Where is Jesus?

(Luke 2:41-52)

At the crossroads Sarah stopped and said, "There's still no sign of James, Jesus or Reuben."

"Oh, they will be at the back of the crowd," said Joanne as she sat down on a rock.

"James always wants to know more about God," said Sarah, "but I thought he would want to talk with me before we have to leave."

"Oh, I'm sure they won't be long," reassured Joanne.

"Can we wait here for them?" asked Sarah who didn't want to leave without saying goodbye to Jesus and James.

"Yes, we can wait for a little time," said Simon tying his donkey to a bush near the rocks. They drank some water and ate the fruit Joanne had brought with her.

After some time Alphaeus said, "Simon, you, Joanne and Sarah should travel on for a bit with Mary and Joseph. Rhoda and I will wait here for the others. I'm sure James and Reuben will be looking after Jesus. I'll tell James to take Jesus to where you will be at the next camp site. They walk faster than you, so they will catch up soon."

"Yes, I think that will be best," said Rhoda. "We don't have so far to get back to Bethlehem but you will need to find somewhere to stay before the sun sets."

"Jesus may have met up with some of our relatives or friends," said Joseph, "there was quite a group of us travelling together coming from the north to Jerusalem."

"Yes, they have probably met up with some friends," said Simon untying his donkey. "You know what the young ones are like, no awareness of time."

"We will walk on slowly and hopefully they will catch up with us before it gets dark," said Joseph leading his donkey.

Alphaeus and Rhoda waited for James at the crossroads while the others walked slowly down the road. Lots of other travellers passed them on their way home; but no sign of Jesus.

As the sun began to set Joseph decided to stop and wait for Jesus. The others agreed to camp there for the night. They soon found a quiet spot just off the road beside some bushes.

"This is a good place to sleep," said Sarah untying the sleeping mats from the donkey's back.

The little group began to prepare some food while they waited for the others to catch up with them. Many travellers passed by but some decided to stop there for the night too. Mary began to get anxious when she didn't see Jesus among any of the travellers.

"I wonder what's keeping them," Mary said after some time.

"Don't worry Mary, I'm sure Jesus will be with Reuben or with the other men," said Sarah. "We have had such a lovely time. It is truly amazing that we met up with you again."

"I hope we can meet up for next year's Feast of the Passover," said Mary.

Just then Reuben and James arrived with a group of pilgrims.

"Where's Jesus?" asked Mary handing Reuben some water and looking round to see if Jesus was among the other men.

"Is He not with you, Mary?" asked Reuben.

"No. We thought He was with you," said Mary anxiously.

"I thought Jesus was with you boys, Reuben," said Joanne looking worried.

"He was not with us," said James. "I just came to say goodbye to Sarah."

"He may be with some of the other people who have come from Jerusalem," said Joseph. "Look, there are some of the people who travelled with us camped over by the trees. I will go and ask if anyone has seen Jesus."

"When was the last time you saw Jesus?" asked Joanne. "You were supposed to be looking after Him, Reuben."

"I think it was in the Temple," said Reuben wiping his brow as he followed Joseph. James and Sarah discussed the arrangements for their wedding while the others went to enquire about Jesus.

"What's the matter Mary?" asked a friend who had travelled to Jerusalem with Mary and Joseph.

"We can't find my son Jesus," said Mary beginning to cry. "He is only twelve and this is His first visit to Jerusalem."

"The last time I remember seeing Him was in the Temple," said the man. "He was talking with the rabbis. He was asking them some difficult questions."

"Yes," said Reuben, "Jesus was certainly questioning the rabbis. We were all amazed at His understanding. Even James didn't know the answers to some of the questions Jesus was asking."

"The Teachers of the Law were surprised too," said the friend who came from Nazareth.

When they returned to the group, Sarah asked anxiously, "Has anyone seen Jesus?"

"No, no one has seen Him all day," said Joseph looking very worried.

"Where could He be?" cried Mary. "He doesn't know His way about Jerusalem. He may have got lost looking for us. He knew we were returning home today, Joseph didn't He?"

"Yes, I told Him this morning that we would be leaving later today," said Joseph.

"Why did you not make sure He was with you, Joseph?" asked Mary.

"I thought Jesus was with Reuben and James," replied Joseph sadly.

Mary was beside herself with worry now.

"Don't worry, Mary," said Reuben, "I'm sure He's not lost. He must still be in Jerusalem."

Joseph began to untie the donkey. "You may be right Reuben," he said, "we will go back immediately to look for Him."

"I will come with you and help you look for Him," said Reuben. "After all it is our fault that Jesus is not here. We should have made sure He was with us when we left."

"I'll come too and meet up with my parents," said James saying goodbye to Sarah. "I only wanted to see Sarah before we left. I didn't know Jesus was missing."

"We will stay here for the night," decided Simon. "Then we will make our way home. You can get home on your own can't you, Reuben?"

"Yes, Father," replied Reuben helping Joseph load up his donkey.

"Come, Mary," said Joseph, "we'd better start back right away."

"I do hope Jesus is alright," said Joanne as she watched the little group go off into the darkness.

"Mary and Joseph didn't have time to eat. Do you think they have any food with them?" asked Sarah who was also very worried.

"They won't be feeling like eating till they have found Jesus," said Joanne taking some flour out of her basket to make some bread.

"I don't think I will sleep tonight," said Sarah helping her mother hand out the food.

"Nor will I," said Simon, "but I'm sure they will find Jesus."

"Jerusalem is a very busy city," said Joanne. "I do hope He is not lost somewhere."

"We can pray to God to keep Him safe till Mary finds Him," said Sarah sadly.

"Yes, let's all pray, asking God to help," replied Joanne.

The next morning Joanne gathered up their belongings.

"Reuben will make his own way home once they have found Jesus," said Joanne confidently as they made their way back home.

Three days later Reuben arrived home.

"Did they find Jesus?" Sarah asked anxiously.

"Yes," replied Reuben sitting down to rest.

"Where was He?" asked Joanne handing him some water.

Simon came hurrying in when he saw Reuben had returned.

"Is Jesus all right?" Simon asked anxiously. "Did you find Him?"

"After looking all day in Jerusalem we went back to the Temple," began Reuben, "and guess what, Jesus was in the Temple where we had left Him. He was still talking to the Teachers of the Law!"

"What? Jesus was still in the Temple!" said Sarah in surprise.

"What did Mary say to Him?" asked Joanne. "Was she angry with Him?"

"More astonished than angry," said Reuben, taking a drink of water.

"What did Jesus say?" asked Sarah.

"He just said they should not have worried," said Reuben. "He asked them why they were searching for Him."

"What! He asked them why they were searching for Him," repeated Simon in amazement.

"Did Jesus not know that everyone had left Jerusalem?" Joanne asked, astonished at what she heard.

"I don't know," said Reuben. "All Jesus said was that they should have known He would be in His Father's house."

"His Father's house!" repeated Sarah. "Of course, Jesus' Father is God."

"You could be right Sarah," said Reuben. "I never thought of that."

"I wonder what Mary thought about it all," said Joanne.

"Well, it has certainly been an exciting trip to Jerusalem this year," said Simon.

"I wouldn't say exciting," said Joanne handing some bread to Reuben. "It turned out to be more worrying than exciting. We won't forget this trip in a hurry."

"Do you think we will see Jesus, Mary and Joseph next year?" asked Sarah hopefully.

"It would be great if we did," said Joanne with a sigh. "We didn't have time to make any arrangements."

Sarah thought about Jesus for a time then said, "Jesus has grown up to be an interesting person, don't you think? He is mature for His age too."

"Yes, He must be a very intelligent young man to be able to discuss with the priests the way He did," said Reuben thoughtfully.

"I wonder what the future holds for Him," said Joanne quietly.

Story 4 - The Baptism
(Matthew 3:13-17, Mark 1:9-11, & Luke 3:21 & 22)

Sarah and James were married a year after their visit to the Temple in Jerusalem. They went to live in a small village near the River Jordan with Sarah's parents. Eighteen years have passed since they met Jesus in Jerusalem when He was twelve years old. Sarah and James now have two children, Rachel aged nine and Benjamin who is seven. Jesus' cousin John lives nearby and preaches to the people beside the River Jordan.

Early one morning Sarah was sitting outside her door busily grinding the corn. Rachel was helping her by pouring the corn into the small hole in the big stone. Benjamin and his father James were taking some sticks to the wood pile behind their house. When James saw Sarah by the door he stopped and said, "I think I will go and see John the Baptist today. I have heard people talking about him. John says we all need to repent and be baptised."

"What does repent mean?" asked Rachel looking up at her father.

"It means saying sorry to God," he replied.

"Why do you need to say sorry to God, Father?" asked Rachel putting her handful of corn back in the bowl.

Before James could answer, Benjamin asked, "Can we come too?"

"Oh, Father, can we come with you, please?" repeated Rachel who always wanted to know what was going on, just like her mother Sarah.

"When were you thinking of going?" asked Sarah standing up.

"Can we go now?" suggested Benjamin. "We can get there and back in a day if we go now."

"Oh, yes let's go now," said Rachel excitedly.

"You're not too busy today are you?" asked James shooing the hens away from the door.

Sarah thought for a while then lifted the grinding stone and went into the house. The children followed hoping for another adventure.

"Oh, please say we can go with Father today, Mother," pleaded Rachel.

Sarah put the grinding stone onto a ledge in the wall and emptied the flour she had ground into a large pot by the small window. The children watched her put away the things she had been using.

"Have you baked some bread today?" asked James standing by the door with the sticks still in his arms.

"I have baked enough bread," said Sarah wiping her hands, "and I have ground all the flour I will need for tomorrow, so I suppose we could go to the River Jordan and hear what John is saying."

"Oh, that's great," said Rachel jumping up and down.

"I'll get some food ready," said Sarah. "James, have you finished putting all the sticks on the wood pile?"

"Yes," said James, "this is the last bundle."

"I'll get some water from the well," suggested Rachel lifting a pot and going towards the door.

"Wait for me, Rachel. I'll come with you after I have put these sticks on the wood pile," said Benjamin hurrying out of the door with his sticks.

"Thank you," replied Mother.

Soon the little family were on the road to the River Jordan. Rachel and Benjamin ran on in front anxious to get there. Many other people were also travelling along the road. Rachel ran back to her mother.

"Are all these people going to listen to John too?" she asked.

"Yes," replied James, "John is a great preacher. He is telling us all to worship God and repent of our sins."

"What sins have you to say sorry for?" asked Benjamin joining his family.

"Sometimes we forget to say thank you to God for all the wonderful things He has done for us," said Sarah.

"And sometimes we do things that we know are wrong so we need to say sorry to God," said James.

"Why do people call him John the Baptist?" asked Benjamin.

"Because he baptises people, silly," replied Rachel laughing.

"What does John do when he baptises people?" asked Benjamin.

James explained that a person goes into the water and John puts them under the water. This is so show that the person wants God to wash away their sin.

"Just like when we get washed and we are all clean again," said Rachel skipping along the path.

"Something like that," laughed James.

"Look. There's the River Jordan," shouted Rachel running down towards the water's edge.

"What a lot of people have come to hear John," said Benjamin in surprise. "Even the Pharisees are here too. Do they need to repent and be baptised?"

"John certainly seems to think so," said James. "Let's go over to where John is talking to the crowd. We can hear what he is saying."

"Stay close to us," warned Sarah. "We don't want you to get lost among all these people."

As they came near, Rachel noticed John standing in the water baptising someone. She wanted to get nearer to see what was happening. So she ran along the edge of the river to where John was. Sarah, James and Benjamin joined her. They watched as John carefully lowered the man under the water then lifted him back out of the water again. When John was standing by the side of the River, Rachel whispered to her mother, "What strange clothes John is wearing!"

"His clothes are made of camel's hair," explained Sarah. "That's why they look different."

John began to talk to the people again when he suddenly stopped and pointed to a man coming towards him.

"What's John saying?" asked Benjamin as they watched the man coming towards them.

"He said that this person is the 'Lamb of God'" said James in surprise.

Everyone stared at the figure standing beside John. They saw Him go into the water with John. As the man came out of the water they heard a sound like someone speaking.

"Look," said Rachel, "there's a dove flying over that man's head."

"I heard a voice saying, 'You are My Son'," said James quietly.

"It's, it's Jesus," whispered Sarah.

"Who?" asked Rachel.

"Jesus! He's our friend we knew when He was a young boy," replied her mother thrilled at the thought of meeting Jesus again. "He has grown up and is now a man."

"Is He the Jesus you told us about?" asked Benjamin. "Is He the baby Jesus who was born in your cave, Mother?"

"The Jesus you met in Jerusalem, Father, when He was twelve years old?" asked Rachel excitedly.

"Yes, yes it is our Jesus," shouted Sarah in amazement.

"Wow," said Benjamin, "Your friend Jesus is being baptised by John."

"Imagine us being here the very day Jesus was coming to be baptised," said Rachel. "Can we go and meet Him?"

"Yes, we will go and speak to Jesus later. He is busy talking to John just now," said Sarah. "Come on; let's have something to eat while we wait."

Rachel and Benjamin were very excited. They had heard all about how Jesus had been born in the cave and about the gifts the Wise Men brought to Him. They even remembered hearing about the time Jesus stayed behind in the Temple in Jerusalem and everyone thought that

Jesus was lost. Their father had blamed himself for not making sure that Jesus was with them. They liked the part when Jesus was found.

Later that day Sarah and James went to introduce themselves to Jesus.

"Jesus, Jesus is it really You?" said Sarah excitedly as she ran up to Him.

"Sarah, James, Shalom!. How wonderful to meet you here," said Jesus as they greeted each other. "And who is this?" asked Jesus, smiling at Rachel as she came shyly up to meet Him. Benjamin stood close to his father.

"This is our daughter Rachel and this is Benjamin," said Sarah introducing the children to Jesus.

"I am so pleased to meet you Rachel, and you too Benjamin," said Jesus putting His arms round the children.

"We have heard all about You, Jesus," said Rachel.

"Our parents have told us You are very special," said Benjamin proudly.

"Are You really special?" asked Rachel as they all sat down on the grass beside the River. Jesus sat beside Rachel.

"Yes, Rachel," said Jesus, "I have come to tell people how to live the way God wants them to."

"Will You come and stay with us?" asked Rachel who wanted Jesus to be her friend too.

"I would like to come to your house Rachel, but I have to go and tell other people about God's Kingdom," said Jesus putting His arm round Rachel's shoulder.

"Where are You going from here Jesus?" asked Sarah.

"I'm going to Galilee to preach the Good News to the people there," replied Jesus standing up. James got up quickly as he wanted to talk to Jesus before He left.

Rachel and Benjamin went to play with the other children who had come with their parents to the River Jordan. James and Sarah talked with Jesus for some time. Then it was time to leave.

"I must go now," said Jesus lifting Rachel up in the air and spinning round with her. Rachel laughed and gave Jesus a hug when He put her down on the ground.

"I don't want You to go," said Rachel sadly. "I wish we could go with You, Jesus. Will we see You again?"

"I'm sure we will meet up again soon Rachel," said Jesus with a knowing smile.

Jesus began to walk away when James shouted, "Jesus, I want to be baptised before we help You with Your work for God."

"Good, do that," replied Jesus turning round. "We'll meet up later in Nazareth."

"Does that mean our parents are going to help You with Your work, Jesus?" asked Benjamin in surprise.

"Can we be Your helpers too?" asked Rachel excitedly.

"Yes," said Jesus, "You can be My helpers too."

"When?" asked Benjamin running after Jesus.

"When we are all ready," replied Jesus as He began to walk away.

They watched Jesus go off by Himself towards the desert.

That same day James and Sarah were baptised by John. As they went home they discussed how they could help Jesus in His work.

"I can't believe Jesus wants us to be His helpers," said Benjamin happily.

"When will we go to help Jesus, Mother?" asked Rachel.

"Soon, children, we will meet up with Jesus soon," promised Sarah.

That night as Rachel and Benjamin were getting ready to go to sleep, Sarah was singing happily to herself.

"Why are you so happy tonight, Mother?" asked Rachel lying down on her sleeping mat.

"I am happy because we met Jesus today," replied Sarah.

"But why is that making you happy?" asked Benjamin covering himself with his blanket.

"You know that we have always said that Jesus is special," explained their mother. "Well, today we understood why He is special."

"Was that because we heard the voice saying that Jesus is God's Son?" asked Benjamin.

"Yes, that was God's voice telling us that Jesus is His Son and that we are to listen to what He says," continued Sarah.

James came over and sat down on the floor beside his children and said, "Jesus has asked us to follow Him and help with His work for God. That means we have to go where He goes."

"How can we help Jesus?" asked Rachel sleepily.

"Are we leaving our house and going away forever?" asked Benjamin excitedly.

"Yes, we will be leaving soon," James told his children.

"Mother, you can help Jesus by preparing food for Him at the end of each busy day," suggested Rachel.

"Yes, Rachel," replied her father. "Now that we know Jesus is the Son of God, we want to be involved in bringing about God's Kingdom."

Story 5 - Jesus Chooses His Twelve Disciples
Chapter One - The Journey to Nazareth
(Matthew 4:12; Luke 4:14-16.)

Sarah and James had met Jesus at the River Jordan. They were happy that Jesus had asked them to help Him. After praying about what to do, they decided to leave their home and follow Jesus. Their children, Rachel and Benjamin, were excited about this new adventure. They wanted to be Jesus' helpers too.

Sarah, James and the children are going to Nazareth to meet up with Jesus. They are preparing to leave.

"When are we going?" Rachel asked her mother. She was bored waiting for her parents to pack up all their belongings.

"We won't be long now Rachel, I just need to make sure we have taken everything with us," replied her mother handing Rachel a basket full of clay pots and wooden plates. Sarah lifted the pile of sleeping mats and took them out of the house. Rachel carried the basket outside and put it on the ground. Sarah shook each mat before rolling it up. Then she put the mats together into a bundle and tied a rope round them. She laid the mats on the ground beside the other bags, baskets and bundles of clothes.

"Why is it taking so long?" Benjamin asked Rachel as he threw some pebbles across the street. He was sitting on the ground guarding their belongings. "I can't wait to see Jesus again."

"Mother says it won't be long now Benjamin," replied Rachel going to the door to look into the empty house.

Benjamin jumped up when he saw his father appear round the corner of the house pulling the donkey behind him.

"I hope the donkey will be able to carry all these things," said Benjamin looking at the bundles.

"Hold the donkey for me please, Benjamin," said James, "while I tie everything onto the donkey's back."

"I can hold the donkey for you, Father," suggested Rachel hoping to hurry things along. "Benjamin can help you lift the bundles and tie them onto the donkey."

"Thank you Rachel," said her father handing over the reins. James tied a strong rope round the donkey's middle, then Benjamin handed his father one of the bundles which he tied securely onto the saddle. Soon everything had been loaded onto the donkey.

"Don't forget the goatskin of water, Sarah," James shouted through the open door.

Sarah came out of the house with a brush in her hand.

"Oh dear, I nearly forgot the water," said Sarah. "Benjamin, can you get it for me? I left the goatskin hanging on the back wall to keep it cool."

She finished sweeping the dirt onto the street as Benjamin came out of the house carrying the goatskin of water.

"That's everything cleared out now," said Sarah closing the door behind Benjamin. Benjamin gave the goatskin to his father who tied it to the rope at the donkey's side. Sarah handed him the brush which he pushed through the bundles making sure it wouldn't fall out.

"Let's get going," he said giving the donkey a gentle pat to make it move.

Rachel and Benjamin ran along the dusty road. James followed leading the heavily-laden donkey, while Sarah walked behind the donkey to make sure nothing fell off.

"How long will it take us to reach Nazareth?" asked Rachel after some time.

"Oh, it's a long way," said James, "It should take us about five or six days depending on how tired you two get."

"Will we stop at an Inn soon?" asked Benjamin who was already feeling tired.

"Yes, when we reach the next village we will stop for the night," replied his father.

Several days later the family arrived in Nazareth just as the sun was beginning to set. They saw some women gathering at the well. Jesus had told them that He was living in Nazareth with His mother Mary and His brothers and sisters.

"We might find Mary at the well," suggested Sarah, "if not, I'm sure one of the women will know where Jesus lives."

Rachel followed her mother as she made her way to the well, while Benjamin and James waited by the side of the road with the donkey.

"Can you tell me where the Carpenter's house is?" Sarah asked one of the women coming from the well with her jar of water on her head.

The lady pointed to some houses below them. "It's the last house on the corner," she told Sarah. Rachel ran to tell her father that the house was nearby. The children hurried on in front. When they found the house, they ran into the courtyard shouting, "Jesus, Jesus!"

"Shalom, Rachel and Benjamin," said Jesus looking up from sawing a large plank of wood. The children ran to greet Him. Jesus put down the saw and swept Rachel up in His arms. "You found us!" said Jesus happily. "It is so good to see you both again."

When she heard the children's voices, Mary came hurrying out of the house wiping her hands on a cloth.

"Welcome to our home," she said with a smile. "I am so pleased to meet you. You must be Sarah's children."

"Yes, I'm Rachel and this is my brother Benjamin," replied Rachel as Jesus put her down.

"Shalom, Mary," shouted Sarah as she came into the courtyard. The two women greeted each other.

"It is so good to see you," said Mary showing Sarah into the house. "You must be tired and hungry from the journey, come in and rest. I have just finished making some goat's cheese."

James arrived pulling the tired donkey. Jesus warmly welcomed James to His home.

"Let Me help you unload your belongings, James," said Jesus. "Then Benjamin can take the donkey to the field at the back of the house."

That night everyone enjoyed a meal together. After Rachel and Benjamin had gone to sleep, Jesus said, "I am ready to leave now as I have to do My Father's work. When I was with My cousin John at the River Jordan, I met a man called Andrew. He is a fisherman from Capernaum. He and his brother Simon are followers of John. I have arranged to meet them in Capernaum."

"We are ready to go whenever You are going," said James.

When the meal was over Sarah helped Mary clear up.

"I've decided to go with Jesus too," said Mary. "Other members of the family will look after our carpenter's business. I will meet up with you at Capernaum in a couple of days. I am so glad you and James are going with Jesus."

The following day, James and his family travelled with Jesus to Capernaum. They found somewhere to live and Sarah cooked the meals for Jesus and her family.

Chapter Two – Jesus Chooses Four Fishermen

(Matthew 4:18-22; Mark 1:16-20; Luke 5:2-11.)

Rachel and Benjamin liked living in Capernaum. They had met some of the fishermen who worked by the Sea of Galilee. Jesus had introduced the children to Andrew and his brother Simon. The children also knew John and his brother James and their father Zebedee who also had a fishing boat. They could recognise whose boat was out fishing. When Jesus talked to the people, James, Rachel and Benjamin were among the crowd listening to Him.

One morning, not long after they had come to live in Capernaum, Rachel and Benjamin wandered down to the shore hoping to talk to the fishermen as they mended their nets.

"Look, over there," said Benjamin, "Simon and his brother Andrew are in their boat. They are casting their net into the water."

"Fishermen don't go out fishing at this time of day," said Rachel, pleased that she had learned something about fishing since she had come to Capernaum.

"You're right, they usually go out at night," said Benjamin. "Maybe they didn't catch any fish last night."

"They didn't bring us any fish this morning so they couldn't have caught anything," said Rachel. "Maybe they are trying again now to catch some fish."

"There's Jesus," shouted Rachel, noticing Jesus standing by the water's edge calling to the fishermen. "I wonder what He is saying to Simon and Andrew."

The children watched as Simon and Andrew hauled the net out of the water and rowed the boat to the shore. As soon as they landed, the two fishermen left their boat and went with Jesus. They watched Jesus go further along the shore and stop beside Zebedee's boat.

"Look, Jesus is talking to James and John," said Benjamin, as they hurried along the shore trying to catch up with Jesus. When they reached Zebedee's boat Jesus had gone. Only the old man was sitting in his boat looking rather surprised.

"Where has everyone gone?" Rachel asked Zebedee.

"You're not going to believe this," replied Zebedee. "They have gone with Jesus and left me here mending the nets."

Later that day the children went back to talk to Zebedee and found that James and John had returned to help their father. A large crowd had gathered on the shore so the children went over to see if Jesus was there. They noticed Simon and Andrew washing their nets at the water's edge. Then the children saw Jesus in the middle of the crowd. The people were crowding round Jesus so He got into Simon's boat, which was pulled up on the shore. Jesus asked him to push the boat out into the water.

The children listened to Jesus as He taught the people from the boat. When Jesus had finished speaking, the crowd began to move away. As the children waited for Jesus to come ashore, Benjamin noticed that the boat was going further out into the water.

"What's happening now?" asked Rachel jumping up and down trying to see what was going on out on the Lake.

"They are going fishing," said Benjamin in surprise, "I can see Simon casting his net into the deep water."

The children watched the little boat bobbing up and down in the water.

"They're pulling in the net," said Benjamin after a few minutes.

"Already?" said Rachel in amazement.

"Yes," said Benjamin. "Look, they're shouting to James and John to come with their boat to help them."

"Oh, I think the boats are going to sink," said Rachel as she watched the boats getting lower in the water as they hauled the net full of fish into the boats.

As the two boats came to the water's edge, Andrew and John jumped into the water and began to haul the boats up onto the beach. Other men hurried to help them. Everyone was astonished to see that both boats were full of fish! Simon and all the people were overwhelmed when they counted their catch.

"Here Benjamin, take some fish to your mother," said Andrew throwing two big fish onto the shore near where the children were standing.

"Wow, look at all the fish," said Rachel. "I've never seen so many."

Benjamin picked up one of the fish. "Wait till Mother sees this," he said handing the fish to Rachel. "Hold it in both hands. Be careful, it's very slippery."

Benjamin picked up the other fish and they carefully carried them home.

"Mother, Mother, look what we have," shouted Rachel as they came into the house.

"Where did you get these fish?" asked Sarah in surprise. "I was told they hadn't caught any fish last night. Not even a small one."

"You'll never believe it," began Benjamin. "You're right; Simon had been fishing all night and had caught nothing. Then, Jesus told Simon to cast his net into the sea and they caught so many fish that James and John had to bring their boat to help them. They had so many fish their net nearly broke."

"Now we will have a good meal tonight won't we Mother?" added Rachel.

"Yes, I will prepare something special," replied Sarah. "Mary should be arriving today. We can have a party to celebrate."

"Can we invite Simon and Andrew?" asked Rachel who always enjoyed a party.

"And James and John too?" added Benjamin.

"Yes, go and invite them to our house tonight," said Sarah. "It will be good for Mary to meet Jesus' new friends."

Mary arrived that evening and was introduced to the fishermen Jesus knew. After the meal, Andrew told everyone that he and Simon were not going to be fishermen any more. Jesus had called them to follow Him.

Simon stood up and announced proudly, "Jesus gave me a new name, and now I am called Peter!"

"That means Rock," Jesus whispered to Benjamin.

"We are going to be fishing for people now," laughed Andrew.

"Jesus also called us to be His followers," said John. "My brother James and I are going to go with Jesus wherever He goes."

"But what about your fishing boats?" inquired Benjamin.

"We have left our father Zebedee in charge of the boats," explained John. "There are plenty of men he can hire to help him."

The following day Peter invited Jesus and His mother to stay at his house. Peter lived in a big house by the sea with his wife Esther and her mother Ruth. The children were surprised when Peter invited them to stay in his house too.

"We have plenty of room and my wife will be happy to have you stay with us from now on. We have a big room You can use as our meeting place, Jesus," Peter told them all.

Everyone was excited that Peter, Andrew, James and John had been chosen to become Jesus' followers too. Mary smiled quietly to herself; her Son's mission had begun.

That night as everyone settled down to sleep Benjamin whispered to Rachel, "That makes five disciples so far."

"Nine if you count us, Mother and Mary," replied Rachel happily.

"I can't wait to go to Peter's house," said Benjamin. "I know his house is the big one down by the shore."

"It will be great all of us living together," announced Rachel as she lay down on her mat. "Maybe Peter's wife Esther will be a follower too!"

Chapter Three – Jesus Calls Two More Disciples

(John 1:43-51)

The next day Sarah, James and Mary went with Jesus and His disciples to Bethsaida. Rachel and Benjamin were excited that they were allowed to go too.

"Bethsaida is the town where Andrew and I grew up," Peter told Benjamin as they walked along the road.

"Perhaps we will meet our friend Philip there," said Andrew. "We all went to the synagogue school together."

As they were going along the shore they did meet Philip. Before Peter could introduce Jesus to Philip, Jesus said to him, "Come, follow Me, Philip."

"Wow, Jesus has asked Peter's friend to be a follower too," Benjamin whispered to Rachel as Philip joined the group.

When they arrived at the village of Bethsaida they made their way to the well for a drink. Suddenly some people began to gather round wanting to talk with Jesus. As Jesus began to walk towards the shore lots of people followed Him. Soon there was a large crowd of people standing on the shore. Jesus sat on a grassy bank and began to talk to the crowd.

Philip, James, Sarah and the children were still at the well getting some water. "I must go and find my friend Nathanael and tell him about Jesus," Philip told James excitedly.

James decided to go with Philip as he wanted to get to know this newest member of the group. Sarah needed to go to the village to get some food but the children didn't want to go with her.

"Father, can we go with you and Philip?" asked Rachel hopefully. "We'd prefer that to shopping with Mother."

"Yes, you can come with us," replied Philip with a laugh.

When they arrived at the market Sarah went shopping and Philip began to look for his friend. He asked several of the stall keepers if they had seen Nathanael but no one had seen him all day.

"I wonder where Nathanael is," Philip said after some time. He sat down by a fruit stall and wiped his brow. It was hot and he had been hurrying through the narrow streets hoping to find his friend. James and the children sat on the ground to rest too.

"Have you seen Nathanael today?" Philip asked the stall owner.

"No, he has not come to the village today as far as I know," replied the man handing Philip some pieces of melon for the children.

"Thank you," said Philip, "I think we all need some refreshment. It's very hot."

The stall keeper cut up more melon and gave it to Philip and James. Philip handed Rachel some coins. She handed the money to the stall owner thanking him for the melon.

"I really want to find Nathanael today," said Philip, "I can't wait to tell him about Jesus."

"I wonder why Philip is so keen to tell his friend about Jesus," whispered Rachel to Benjamin as they enjoyed the cool juicy melon.

"I was wondering that too," replied Benjamin. "After all he could see him another day."

After they had eaten the melon, Philip stood up. He decided that they should get back to the others.

"I don't think Nathanael is coming to the market today. He lives in Cana which is too far away for us to go and find him. Come on you two, we had better get going."

"I'll let Nathanael know you were looking for him," shouted the stall owner as they left.

As they passed the synagogue on their way back, Philip noticed his friend sitting under the shade of a fig tree reading.

"Nathanael! Nathanael! I have been looking for you everywhere," shouted Philip running up to him. Nathanael stood up and greeted his friend.

"What's the matter Philip?" asked Nathanael calmly.

"Nathanael, I have some great news for you," replied Philip excitedly, "I have found the One Moses wrote of in the Law, the One preached about by the prophets."

"Who?" asked Nathanael wondering why Philip was so excited.

"Jesus, it's Jesus, Joseph's son, Jesus from Nazareth!" explained Philip.

Nathanael looked at Philip and said, "Nazareth? Can anything good come from there?"

"Come and see for yourself," said Philip taking Nathanael by the arm. As they walked along the road Philip introduced his friend to James and the children.

Benjamin and Rachel had to run to keep up with Philip who was hurrying along the road. On the way Philip explained to Nathanael how Jesus had asked him to be His follower as soon as He had seen him. As they arrived at the shore they saw that Jesus was still preaching to the crowd.

When Jesus saw Philip bringing his friend to meet Him, Jesus stopped talking, stood up and looked at Nathanael.

"Here is a true Israelite in whom there is nothing false," said Jesus as they came up to Him.

"How do You know anything about me?" asked Nathanael in surprise.

"I saw you while you were still under the fig tree before Philip found you," Jesus answered. Nathanael was amazed.

"Rabbi, You are the Son of God, the King of Israel!" he exclaimed.

Jesus decided to stay a few days in Bethsaida. That night as the children were getting ready to go to sleep, Rachel told her mother about finding Nathanael and how Jesus knew all about him.

"It's getting so exciting," said Rachel as she watched her mother lay the sleeping mats on the floor. "I wonder how many people Jesus will choose to be His special followers."

"It's wonderful being a part of Jesus' work," said Sarah as she covered Benjamin with a blanket. "I can't wait to see who else Jesus will choose to join us."

"That makes seven counting Father," said Benjamin naming the disciples.

"And don't forget Mother, Mary and us as well," said Rachel jumping up and dancing on her mat.

"Yes, we are all Jesus' disciples but I think these seven men are special to Jesus," said Sarah trying to get Rachel to lie down again.

"What does it mean to be a disciple," asked Benjamin, "what is a disciple?"

"Us," replied Rachel with a laugh. "Disciples are people who follow someone and we are followers of Jesus."

"Yes, Rachel, you are right but I think it means more than that," said Sarah thoughtfully. "Why don't you ask Jesus Benjamin? He will know what it means."

"I'll ask Jesus tomorrow," said Benjamin sleepily.

Chapter Four – The Final Five Disciples

(Matthew 9:9-13 & 10:1-4; Mark 2:13-18 & 3:13-21;
Luke 5:27-31 & 6:12-16.)

The next day Benjamin found Jesus on His own, sitting quietly by the water's edge.

"Can I ask You a question Jesus?" said Benjamin sitting down beside Him.

"Yes of course you can, Benjamin" replied Jesus. "What is it you want to know?"

"Well, You have chosen seven men to be Your special helpers," Benjamin began. "You call them Your disciples. What is a disciple?"

"That is a good question," replied Jesus putting His arm round Benjamin's shoulder. "A disciple is someone who is willing to learn from the person they are following. I need men to listen to what I am saying, believe it is the truth and learn from Me. When I leave this world these disciples will carry on the work I have started. I have called these men to follow Me and they have left everything to come with Me. I will teach them all they need to know so that they can carry on after I have gone."

Benjamin didn't want to ask Jesus what He meant by saying when He had gone. He got up thanked Jesus and went home to tell his mother what Jesus had said. Sarah was worried about Jesus saying He was leaving but she put that thought out of her mind. She was happy to know that the disciples would learn from Jesus about God's Kingdom and His love for everyone who believes. Then they could tell others about Jesus.

Some days later Jesus and His followers went back to Capernaum. As they were walking through the town Peter pointed to a man sitting at a table counting his money. "That's Matthew collecting the taxes for the Romans," he told the children. Benjamin noticed a Roman soldier standing beside Matthew guarding the money. Suddenly a group of people came along shouting at Matthew, "Cheat, cheat, you charge us too much tax."

"Imagine working for the Romans," shouted an old man shaking his fist at the tax collector.

The Roman soldier stepped forward and threatened the people with his sword. The people moved off still shouting.

"Why do the people not like tax collectors?" asked Rachel as they watched the people hurry away.

"Everyone knows Matthew adds on extra money for himself," explained Andrew who was standing beside the children. "Tax collectors work for the Roman government, that's another reason no one likes them."

"And they are very rich aren't they Andrew?" added Benjamin.

"Yes, they are very rich because they take more money than they have to, from both poor and rich people," Andrew replied.

Just then Jesus went over to the table where Matthew was writing in a book.

"Come along with Me," Jesus told him. Immediately Matthew got up, left the Roman soldier to look after his money and followed Jesus.

"Wow, imagine Jesus wanting a tax collector to be one of His followers," said Rachel in surprise.

As they were making their way through the streets Matthew said, "I would like to invite You to my house for a dinner party."

"Thank you for inviting us Matthew, we will come to your house tonight," replied Jesus.

When Benjamin heard this he whispered quietly, "I wonder why Jesus would want to go to a tax collector's house to eat."

Rachel and Benjamin wanted to go and see Matthew's house but their father wouldn't let them.

"Go and tell your mother that she doesn't need to prepare the evening meal for us all as we will be eating at Matthew's house tonight," James told them.

Rachel and Benjamin were disappointed that they couldn't go to the special dinner. They hurried home and told their mother all about Jesus choosing Matthew to be another of His disciples.

"Why do you think Jesus chose such a bad person to be His follower too?" asked Rachel as they sat and ate their meal. Just then James came hurrying into the house to wash and get ready to go to the meal at Matthew's house.

"Jesus must know that Matthew will change to be a better person," Sarah replied handing James a bowl of water. "Maybe he isn't totally bad."

"Was Jesus happy to go to Matthew's house, Father?" asked Benjamin.

"Yes, Jesus doesn't mind eating with disreputable characters," replied James drying his face. "In fact He wants to be friends with everyone."

"Can we go with Father and watch the people arriving at Matthew's house, please?" pleaded Rachel after they had finished eating.

"We won't get in the way," promised Benjamin, "and we will come right back after everyone has gone into the house."

Sarah agreed to let the children go and watch the people arrive. When they got to Matthew's house Rachel noticed how big it was with a lovely courtyard built round the house. James left the children by the side of Matthew's house and went in. The children stood by the wall of the courtyard waiting for the others to arrive.

"Look at all these people who have been invited to the meal," said Benjamin. "Do you think they are tax collectors too? They must be Matthew's friends. Jesus doesn't seem to mind being with them."

"The Pharisees don't look too happy about it," said Rachel noticing many religious leaders whispering together outside Matthew's house.

"I hope Father will tell us all about the dinner party tomorrow," said Rachel as they walked home.

The next day Rachel woke up early so that she could ask her father all about the big party at Matthew's house.

"We saw lots of men going to the party," said Rachel. "Were they all tax collectors? Was Jesus happy eating and talking to them?"

"Yes, He was," replied James. "You see, Jesus loves people and He wants everyone to be part of His kingdom."

"We saw some Pharisees outside Matthew's house. Did they say anything about Jesus?" asked Benjamin.

"They didn't think Jesus was a very good example to us by eating and drinking with crooks," explained James, "Jesus asked them if healthy people or the sick needed a doctor."

"Sick people need a doctor," answered Rachel quickly.

"Quite right Rachel," said James. "Sick people need a doctor and sinful people need Jesus. Jesus told them that He had come to call sinners to repent."

"Oh!" said Benjamin in surprise. Benjamin thought about this for a while then asked "What does repent mean again?"

"It means being sorry for not doing what God wants," explained James, "I suppose Jesus choses people who are prepared to change their wrong ways of behaving and thinking."

"That's right," said Sarah, "we are all bad sometimes but so long as we are sorry and want Jesus to change us to be better people, that's what He wants."

"And He wants us to believe that He is God's Son," said Benjamin quietly.

"Yes, Benjamin," answered James, "that is who He is."

"I believe Jesus is the Son of God and very special," replied Rachel.

James said, "Let's thank God for sending Jesus and for our new friend Matthew who is now one of us."

Sometime later Jesus went up a mountain by Himself to pray. He prayed all night and the next day He selected four more men to be His special disciples. They were Thomas, Simon the Zealot, Judas, also known as Thaddaeus and Judas Iscariot. (Nathanael is also known as Bartholomew.)

Story 6 - The Happy Wedding

(John 2:1-11)

Jesus was now about thirty years old and was living in Capernaum. He had chosen twelve of His followers, including James, to be His special disciples. Jesus' mother Mary, Sarah, Rachel and Benjamin were also among His followers. They all lived together in Peter's house in Capernaum.

One day Sarah and her family were getting ready to go to a wedding. Rachel was very excited as she had never been to a wedding before. The wedding was to take place in a little village called Cana. Jesus, Mary and the disciples were going to the wedding too. Nathanael, one of Jesus' disciples, came from Cana so they were going to stay at his house.

"When are we leaving?" asked Rachel as she watched her mother pack up their things.

"I'm almost ready," said Sarah. "Go and see if your father has brought the donkey from the field Rachel, and tell Benjamin we will be leaving soon."

Rachel ran out of the house and bumped into Mary coming out of the door. "Oh Mary, are you ready to leave?" asked Rachel, "We are waiting to load up the donkey."

"Yes, we have packed up all we will need," said Mary. "Jesus is waiting for us at the end of the road."

Soon everyone was ready. James tied the bundles onto the donkey and they set off for Cana.

When they arrived at Cana, there was great excitement as everyone had been invited to the wedding. The villagers had been preparing for weeks. The celebration feasts had been going on for several days. Now it was the day of the wedding ceremony. As they walked along the street they passed the house where the bride was waiting for her groom to arrive. Mary and Sarah joined some friends who were standing under a tree talking. Rachel and Benjamin ran off to play with the other children while Nathanael took James to his house. When he got there he unloaded their belongings and returned to where Jesus had met up with the men of the village. Sarah took the children to Nathanael's house to get ready for the wedding.

"Children, I have a surprise for you," said Sarah picking up one of the bundles James had left. Rachael ran over to her mother and watched as she opened the bundle.

"Oh, what a pretty dress," said Rachel touching the beautiful blue material. "Are you going to wear it to the wedding?"

"Yes," replied Sarah, "and I have made a new dress for you too. Shut your eyes."

Rachel shut her eyes tightly and put her hands over her face so that she couldn't see anything.

"Can I open my eyes yet?" asked Rachel impatiently.

"In a minute," said her mother unfolding the new dress.

"There, now you can open your eyes."

Rachel took her hands from her face.

"Oh, Mother it's beautiful, just like your blue one," she exclaimed as she took the new dress and held it up. "Can I try it on?"

"Of course you can," replied her mother, "you are to wear it today for the wedding but you need to get washed first."

Rachel hurriedly took off her tunic, washed her face, hands and feet then put on the new dress.

"It fits perfectly," she said running about the room showing Benjamin her new dress.

"Can I go and show Jesus my new dress?" Rachel asked.

"Yes, but don't be a nuisance if Jesus is talking to the people," said Sarah.

"Can I go too?" asked Benjamin.

"Wait a minute Benjamin, you need to wash and put on your new clothes too," said Sarah taking out a new white tunic for Benjamin.

"Oh thank you Mother," said Benjamin hurriedly washing his hands and feet. He dressed quickly, put on his sandals then hurried out the door, after Rachel.

"Stay with Jesus," shouted Sarah brushing her hair. "I'll be along soon."

Rachel and Benjamin ran off to find Jesus. They saw Him sitting on a wall beside a house.

"Jesus, are You ready to go to the wedding?" asked Rachel as she ran up to Him.

"Shalom Rachel, yes I am ready for the wedding. How pretty you look. I like your dress, is it a new one?" Jesus asked her.

"Yes, Mother made it for me," replied Rachel.

"It's lovely," said Jesus lifting her into the air and spinning round with her.

Just then some other children came running over to Jesus.

"I'm Joshua and this is my sister Anna," said one of the boys. "Have You come for the wedding?"

"It's our sister who is getting married today," said Anna looking at Rachel. The other children gathered round Jesus.

"Can I have a spin round too?" Anna asked Jesus after a time.

"Of course," said Jesus lifting Anna into the air.

"We're all ready to go to the wedding, are You?" asked Joshua.

"Yes, we are just waiting for everyone to arrive," replied Jesus.

"When will the procession start?" asked Rachel taking Jesus' hand. "We can't wait to go to the wedding."

"We will set off soon," said Jesus taking Anna's hand too. "Ah! Here comes your mother, Rachel."

"Come on children, let's see who gets there first," said Jesus starting to run down the street. The boys followed, laughing as they ran. Sarah joined the villagers who were making their way to the groom's house. The groom and his friends then set out from his home to the house of his bride. They were carrying torches as they led the joyful procession through the village. Musicians were playing drums and tambourines, beautifully dressed girls were dancing among the crowd and the children skipped and danced in time to the music.

"Listen to the music," said Rachel excitedly, "It's such a happy tune they are playing."

Soon they arrived at the home of the bride who was waiting with her attendants for her groom to arrive. The house was brightly lit with lots of clay oil-lamps.

Jesus went off with His disciples and the other men. The children joined the women.

After the wedding ceremony was over everyone went back to the groom's house for the feast. Torches and oil-lamps lit the way as the procession walked up the street. When they arrived Rachel noticed that a special canopy had been prepared in the courtyard where the bride and groom were sitting dressed in all their finery. The canopy was decked with beautiful flowers. Bowls of fruit and nuts were placed in front of the happy couple. Soon it was time for the feast to begin. As the guests waited for the food to be served Mary came rushing up to Rachel.

"Have you seen Jesus, Rachel? There's a problem we need to do something about," she whispered.

"The last time I saw Jesus He was still in the courtyard talking to some people," answered Rachel.

"I must find Him," said Mary anxiously looking about her.

Rachel took Mary by the hand and led her to where Jesus was resting against a tree.

"Oh there You are, Jesus," said Mary as she took Him aside. "We have a problem," Mary whispered. "The Master of the Banquet says there is no wine left."

Rachel overheard what they were saying. She followed Mary and Jesus back to the house to see what He would do. Mary stopped beside the servants who were standing by the door and told them to do whatever Jesus told them. Rachel ran off to find her new friends to tell them what had happened.

"It's a secret," whispered Rachel. "You mustn't tell anyone but they have no wine left and everyone is waiting for the meal. Do you think Jesus is going to do something?"

"Come on, let's see what Jesus will do," said Anna excitedly.

"Don't expect He can do anything," Joshua said sulkily. "It isn't His wedding. It's not His problem. I'm hungry. I just want something to eat."

"You don't know Jesus," said Rachel watching the servants.

"Jesus is kind and He likes to help people," added Benjamin.

"Look, two of the servants are carrying some pots," said Rachel hurrying over to the servants who were coming out of the courtyard. The others followed.

"What are you doing?" Joshua asked one of the servants.

"Jesus told us to fill up the six stone jars with water," the servant replied.

"Each one holds over ninety litres," said the other servant. "We filled them with water already this morning. It's going to take some time to fill them again."

"We can help you," offered Benjamin who was always ready to give a helping hand.

"Thanks, that will be a real help," replied the servant handing the children a pot each. "We will need to go to the well several times."

"The guests won't be very pleased to have to drink water for the rest of the evening," said the other servant as they hurried towards the well. "Imagine not having enough wine left for this special feast."

The other servant laughed and said, "They must have finished all the wine last night."

When they got to the well one of the servants pulled up the bucket then Benjamin and Joshua took it in turns to pour the water into the pots. They all carried the pots, full of water, back to the house and emptied them into the six large stone jars that were standing by the door. They had to go to the well three times.

"That should do it," said one of the servants, "I don't think we need any more water."

They all went back to the house each carrying a pot on their head. They poured the water into the jars.

"There, all six of them are full of water," said one of the servants wiping his brow with the back of his hand.

"Go and find Jesus, Joshua and tell Him we have done what He said," the other servant told him. "Oh, and thanks for your help. We would still be there filling up all those jars if you hadn't helped us," he shouted as the children hurried into the house.

When they found Jesus they told Him that all six jars were full to the brim.

Jesus went out and told one of the servants to take some water out of one of the stone jars.

"Now take it to the Master of the Banquet," Jesus told the servant.

So the servant poured some water into a golden jug.

"I wonder what he will say when he tastes the water," whispered Joshua.

"He doesn't know where it came from," said Anna.

"I bet he will spit it out," laughed Joshua.

The children watched as the servant poured the water out of the golden jug into the Master of the Banquet's silver goblet. To their amazement wine poured out of it. The servant took the silver goblet to the Master of the Banquet.

"Sh," whispered Anna. "Look, he's taking a sip."

The man drank from the silver goblet.

"Mmm, this is the best wine I have ever tasted," said the Master of the Banquet. "Imagine the bridegroom keeping the best wine to the last. I'll need to go and speak to him."

He went to speak to the groom with the goblet of wine still in his hand.

The children couldn't wait to tell Mary what had happened.

"I knew Jesus would do something to help," said Mary happily

when the children told her. "Don't tell anyone. The bridegroom will be very embarrassed if everyone knew he didn't have enough wine for the wedding feast."

"We won't tell anyone, promise – it'll be our secret," replied Rachel.

"I can't believe that Jesus actually turned the water into wine," said Joshua in amazement.

"Jesus is someone very special!" said Rachel.

Just then Jesus came over to the children.

"I hear you children have been helping the servants," said Jesus with a chuckle. "Come on, you must be hungry, it's time to eat."

"I am hungry," said Joshua, "but how did You do it Jesus?"

"Don't ask how Jesus did it," said Rachel in an exasperated voice. "Jesus can do anything. Can't You Jesus?"

Jesus smiled and they all went into the house together.

Later on the musicians played and the dancing began. Everyone was having fun.

"This is a good party Joshua," said Rachel. "Come on, let's go and watch the men dancing."

Joshua and Rachel ran over to Jesus.

"I wish we could join in the dancing," said Rachel sadly. The children watched the men dancing in a circle.

After a wonderful party Sarah and James took the children back to Nathanael's house.

"That was the best wedding ever," said Rachel as she lay down to sleep.

"Yes," agreed Benjamin sleepily, "especially when Jesus changed water into wine!"

"Sh," whispered Rachel, "No one knows about our secret."

"What secret?" asked Sarah as she picked up the oil lamp.

"Oh it's nothing," replied Benjamin, "just something that happened at the wedding."

The next day they all returned to Capernaum.

Story 7 - Jesus The Healer
Chapter One - A Man with Leprosy
(Matthew 8:1-4 Mark 1:40-44: Luke 5:12-14.)

After the wedding in Cana, Jesus returned to Capernaum with His twelve disciples and His mother Mary. Sarah and her children, Rachel and Benjamin, went back to Capernaum too. Peter had a large house near the shore where he lived with his wife Esther and her mother Ruth. Peter had offered his house to Jesus as a meeting place. Jesus would preach to the people in that area while staying at Peter's house. Mary, Sarah and her children and the disciples all stayed there too. Many people followed Jesus wanting to listen to what He said.

Every morning, before the sun was up, Jesus would go up the mountain to be alone with God to pray. Often James, Sarah and the children would leave Capernaum early to go and meet up with Jesus to bring Him some bread to eat. One day, as they were walking along the road towards the mountainside, Rachel noticed a group of people in the distance. They were huddled together under a tree out in the countryside.

"Who are these strange looking people sitting outside Capernaum away from everyone?" Rachel asked her mother.

"They are lepers," replied Sarah. Then she warned then, "Never go near anyone who has leprosy. It's a very dangerous disease. If you touch someone with leprosy, you will get it too."

"I saw some people living in the caves in the hills as we travelled here," said Benjamin. "They were dressed in rags. Did they have leprosy?"

"Yes," answered Sarah, "Lepers have to live in the caves away from people. Their families leave food for them outside the caves but they have to wait till everyone has gone before they can come out and get it."

"Does that mean they can't meet their families?" asked Benjamin.

"People with leprosy must be very sad and lonely," said Rachel.

"Yes, I suppose they are sad, Rachel," replied Sarah. "They must only see their families from a distance when they leave the food for them."

"I wouldn't like to have leprosy," said Rachel.

Just then a crowd of people came along the road towards them.

"Ah, that must be Jesus on His way back from praying," said James. "There's always a crowd following Jesus."

"Can we go with Father to give Jesus His breakfast?" asked Rachel anxious to see Jesus and listen to the stories He told.

"Yes, on you go, but remember what I told you about not going near these people with leprosy," warned Sarah handing Rachel some bread wrapped in a cloth. "Come home with your father, as we don't know this town and you might get lost. I'll go back into the village to buy some food."

The children ran ahead making sure they kept away from the little group sitting under the tree. They saw Jesus among the crowd and gave Him the bread.

"Come on, let's go back into Capernaum," said Jesus when He had finished eating. "I want to talk to all these people."

Jesus and James walked in front with Rachel and Benjamin following close behind them. As they came near the men with leprosy, one of them came hurrying over to Jesus. He knelt down right in front of Him. Everyone backed away including Rachel who was afraid of the man.

"Lord, if You are willing, You can make me clean," said the man looking up into Jesus' face.

Jesus, filled with compassion, reached out His hand and touched the man. "I am willing," He said. "Be clean!"

Immediately the man was cured of his leprosy.

"Don't tell anyone," Jesus warned the man. "Go and show yourself to the priest and offer the gift Moses commanded as a testimony to your healing."

"Did you see that," exclaimed Benjamin in amazement. "Jesus touched that leper."

"Yes, I saw Jesus touching him," said Rachel. "Do you think Jesus will get the disease now?"

"No, I don't think so," said Benjamin. "Jesus wanted to help the man and show him and us, not to be afraid."

"I can't wait to tell Mother," said Rachel, "she won't believe Jesus touched a man with leprosy."

Chapter Two - The Roman Centurion's Servant

(Matthew 8: 5-17 & Luke 7:1-10)

Jesus and His disciples entered Capernaum, followed by the crowd who were still talking about Jesus touching the man with leprosy. Rachel and Benjamin kept close to Jesus and their father. Suddenly a Roman centurion came up to Jesus in a panic.

"Lord, my servant is very ill. He lies on his bed in my home. He can't walk," the centurion told Jesus. "He's in terrible pain."

The crowd gathered round Jesus when they saw the centurion speaking to Him. They wanted to see what Jesus would do. Rachel and Benjamin also wondered what would happen.

"Do you think Jesus will go and heal the servant?" whispered Rachel.

Before Benjamin could answer they heard Jesus say to the centurion, "I'll come and heal your servant."

"I hope we can go with Jesus and see the servant being healed," said Rachel excitedly.

"Wait," said Benjamin, "what's the Roman centurion saying?"

When the Roman centurion told Jesus that he didn't deserve to have Him come to his house, Rachel wondered how Jesus was going to heal the servant. She was even more surprised when she heard the centurion say, "Just say the word and my servant will be healed."

Everyone was amazed and waited to see what was going to happen next.

Jesus turned to the crowd and said, "I have not found anyone in Israel with such faith." Looking at the centurion He added, "Go home, your servant is healed just as you believed."

The centurion thanked Jesus and hurried away.

"I wonder if his servant is healed," said Rachel as she watched the centurion march quickly up the street.

Jesus and the crowd move on towards the shore where Jesus sat on a grassy hill and taught the people.

Later that day as Rachel and Benjamin were sitting among the crowd listening to Jesus, Sarah arrived bringing some bread and cheese for them. Benjamin took some food to Jesus. As they sat and ate their lunch Rachel told her mother all about the man with leprosy.

"Jesus touched the man, Mother," said Rachel.

Before Sarah could say anything, Benjamin told her about the Roman centurion wanting Jesus to heal his servant. As he was telling his mother the story James came over to join them.

"Do you think the servant is better now?" Benjamin asked his father.

"I'm sure he is," said James looking over to where Jesus was talking to the people. "Jesus cares for everyone, even servants."

"Seems that includes people with leprosy and Romans too!" added Sarah as she picked up her basket.

Sarah told the children to go along the shore to the fishermen and get some fish. Then she went back home to prepare a meal for Jesus and the disciples. Rachel and Benjamin ran off to get the fish. They found Zebedee beside his boat mending his nets and asked him for some fish. While he gutted the fish the children told him all about the Roman centurion asking Jesus to heal his servant.

"Jesus is amazing isn't He?" said Rachel as she watched Zebedee clean the fish. "I didn't expect Him to help a Roman soldier's servant but He did."

"We may not like Roman soldiers but that centurion must have been very worried about his servant," replied Zebedee. "It couldn't have been easy for him to ask Jesus for help."

"I didn't think about that," said Benjamin. "The Roman centurion isn't a Jew like us, is he? I wonder how he knew Jesus could help him."

"Jesus seems to care for Jews and Gentiles," said Zebedee wrapping the fish in an old piece of net. "Jesus must have known that the centurion believed He could heal his servant."

Rachel and Benjamin played for a while by the shore looking for any interesting things brought up onto the beach by the waves.

"Don't forget your fish," shouted Zebedee to the children as they left to go home.

"Thanks, Zebedee," said Benjamin.

"We'll come and see you another day," Rachel called out as they waved goodbye.

As they walked home through the market stalls they noticed a crowd of people gathered at the end of the street.

"I wonder what's happening over there," said Rachel. "Let's go and see, Benjamin."

The children hurried along the road and pushed their way to the front of the crowd.

"What's going on?" Benjamin asked someone he knew.

The children were told that the centurion's servant had been healed and that the man in the middle of the crowd had seen him.

"Is it true that the servant is better?" Benjamin asked the man.

"Yes," said the man. "I know this Roman centurion. He's a good man; he built our synagogue for us. He is kind and helpful and often discusses things about God with our Jewish elders."

"Did you see the servant?" interrupted Rachel excitedly, "Tell us, please. I want to know how he got better."

"I don't know how it happened," said the man, "I went to see how the servant was feeling and there he was walking about doing his work as usual."

"Had the servant been ill for a long time?" someone asked.

"No, he took ill very suddenly about a week ago but the doctor could do nothing for him," replied the man. "He was a good servant. The centurion was very worried about him. He just got worse and worse and everyone knew that the servant was going to die."

"How did the centurion know Jesus could help him?" Benjamin asked.

"When one of our Jewish elders heard about the servant he told the centurion to go and find Jesus," the man answered. "After all he had nothing to lose had he?"

"But the Roman centurion is a Gentile," said a woman in the crowd. "How did he know Jesus would help a Gentile?"

"He didn't," said the man. "The centurion must have loved his servant and didn't want him to die. So, in desperation, he decided to find Jesus as the Jewish elder told him to."

"When did the servant get better?" asked Rachel who always wanted to know everything. "Did he get up right away or did it take a while for him to feel well again?"

"The very hour that Jesus said he would be healed, the servant felt better again," said the man. "It's a miracle!"

"Wow," said Rachel, "that's amazing. I knew Jesus could make him better, but I thought He would need to touch the servant or at least see him."

"I can't wait to tell Mother that the servant is healed," said Benjamin as they made their way home.

"Imagine, he was healed the minute Jesus said he would be," added Rachel.

Later that night as the children were getting ready to go to sleep James said, "Let's thank God for healing the Roman centurion's servant."

They all agreed and thanked God for healing the servant and the man with leprosy.

Chapter Three – Through the Roof!

(Matthew 9:2-7, Mark 2:3-12 & Luke 5:18-25.)

Sometimes Jesus hadn't time to eat as there were so many people needing His healing. One day Peter's house was full of people and Jesus was telling them about God's kingdom. Rachel and Benjamin were there too, listening to Jesus.

"The people are even standing outside the door," said Sarah as she managed to push through the crowd to bring some water for Jesus to drink.

It was getting hot inside the house and Rachel wanted to go outside but everyone was pushing nearer to Jesus to let more people in.

"What was that?" asked Benjamin as he felt some stones hitting his head.

"Where's all the dust coming from?" said Sarah looking up at the roof.

Suddenly there was a loud crack and more rubble, stones and earth came falling down from the roof.

"What's going on?" asked a woman in alarm as she tried to move away from the falling debris.

The next thing everyone saw was a man being lowered down through the roof. He was lying on a mat held by four ropes. Benjamin looked up and saw four faces peering down through the hole in the roof.

"They've broken Peter's roof!" said Benjamin, "He'll be angry about that."

Jesus said to the man lying on the mat, "Son, your sins are forgiven."

The Teachers of the Law, who were sitting near Jesus, began to mutter to themselves. Jesus turned to them and said, "Why are you thinking these things? Is it easier to tell this paralytic man that his sins are forgiven or to tell him to get up and walk? So that you know the Son of Man has authority on earth to forgive sins…" Jesus turned to the man lying on his mat and said, "I tell you, get up, take your mat and go home!"

Immediately the man got up, rolled up his mat and made his way through the crowd towards the door. The people just stared at the man in astonishment.

"We've never seen anything like this before," said someone as the man walked out of the house. Everyone was amazed and praised God as they left the house. Peter stood in the middle of the room looking up at the hole in his roof. When everyone had gone Esther, Sarah and Ruth started to sweep all the mess out of the house.

"Well, I'm amazed!" said Granny Ruth lifting a big chunk of the roof and carrying it outside.

"Benjamin, bring a basket, please," said Sarah wiping her brow. "Where are we going to put all this mess?"

Just then the four men came into the house and spoke to Peter.

"We are sorry we had to break your roof but it was the only way we could get our friend to Jesus," said one of the men.

"Don't worry, Peter, we will fix it," said another of the men. "We will come back as soon as possible with matting and plaster to sort it."

"We are really sorry for all this mess," said the first man. "Here, let me help you clear up, then we will go and get what's needed to fix your roof."

"Thank you," said Peter still worrying about his roof. The man took the brush from Esther and began to sweep the rubble into a pile. As they were leaving Jesus came back into the house.

"I've never seen such faith," He told the men. "You four men cared for your friend so much that you took the trouble of breaking the roof so that he could be healed."

"It was the only way to get to You, Jesus," replied the man lifting the pile of rubble and putting it into a basket.

Rachel and Benjamin ran to the dump with the basket of rubbish and soon the house was clean again. The men came back with matting, plaster and long lengths of wood. They put some matting across the hole and held it down with some stones. It would take some time to fix the roof properly but in the meantime as least the rain would not get into the house.

It was late in the evening by the time everyone was ready to eat.

"What a day it's been," said Granny Ruth as she sat down beside Jesus.

"It certainly has been a busy day," replied Jesus as he took the bowl of water Rachel had brought to wash His feet. "I'm ready for something to eat. I'm hungry and tired. I could do with a rest."

When she had washed His feet, Jesus laid back on some pillows and shut His eyes.

"Jesus is wonderful isn't He?" whispered Rachel to Granny Ruth as she took the bowl of water away.

"Yes, He is," replied Ruth, "now let's get the food on the table and be thankful our roof is safe tonight and will soon be repaired."

"And thank God that the man can walk," added Rachel as she returned to the room with some freshly baked bread.

"His friends will be happy too, now that he can walk," said Benjamin with a laugh.

"I am thankful too," said Peter. "I'm glad they are sorting my roof."

Chapter Four - Jesus Heals Many People
(Matthew 8:14-15, Mark 1: 29-34 & Luke 4: 38-41.)

It was the Sabbath and all the men had gone with Jesus to the Synagogue. Rachel and Benjamin were sitting quietly by the door of the house. Esther's mother Ruth, who was known to everyone as Granny Ruth, was not feeling well. The children had been sent outside because they were making too much noise.

Sarah opened the door and shouted to the children, "I need more water. Granny Ruth has a fever. Benjamin, will you go to the well for me?" She gave Benjamin the pot she was holding.

"Yes Mother, I'll get you more water," said Benjamin jumping up and taking the pot.

"Take this pot too," said Esther coming to the door and handing him another pot. "Be as quick as you can Benjamin, Granny Ruth is very hot and I need more water to cool her head," she called out.

Rachel followed Esther into the house. She looked at Granny Ruth lying on her mat, moaning. Esther poured the last drop of water onto a cloth and placed the cool cloth on Granny Ruth's hot head. Rachel didn't know what to do. Granny Ruth looked very ill.

"I'll go and see if Jesus is coming," said Rachel after some time. "He will help Granny Ruth."

"Oh dear, the men will be returning home soon and I haven't made the meal yet," said Esther with a sigh, "I have been too busy looking after my mother."

"Here's Benjamin with more water," said Rachel.

"Don't worry; I'll start preparing the meal," said Sarah. "Yes Rachel, go and see if Jesus is on His way home. He will help Granny Ruth."

Benjamin handed Esther the water pots then went over to Granny Ruth.

"You will be alright soon, Granny Ruth," he told her taking her hand, "Rachel has gone to find Jesus. He will help you."

Granny Ruth didn't reply. Her eyes were closed and her body lay stiff on her mat.

As Rachel ran up the street, she met Peter and Andrew coming from the synagogue.

"Peter, where's Jesus?" Rachel asked anxiously, "Granny Ruth is very ill."

Peter hurried to his house to see how his mother-in-law was.

Just then Rachel noticed Jesus coming out of the synagogue, so she ran up to Him.

"Jesus, come quickly, Granny Ruth is sick and can't get up," she told Him taking hold of His hand and pulling Him along the road.

Rachel and Jesus hurried home followed by Andrew, James and John.

When they went into the house, Jesus found Granny Ruth lying on her mat burning up with a fever.

"Can You make her better, Jesus?" pleaded Esther placing another cool, wet cloth on her mother's brow.

Jesus stood beside Granny Ruth; He bent over her and told the fever to leave her. Then He took hold of her hand and helped her up. Immediately the fever left her and Granny Ruth sat up.

"Oh, I'm feeling better now," she said standing up. "Thank You Jesus. Now where's the flour? I need to make some bread. You'll all be hungry."

"Are you sure you are feeling all right?" asked Esther rolling up the mat.

"I'm fine, thanks to Jesus," laughed Granny Ruth, "we can all help to get the meal ready."

Jesus and His disciples sat down at the low table to wait for the meal. Esther and Rachel brought some water for them to wash their feet. Peter whispered to his wife, "Jesus needs to rest; He never stops healing people. Even today in the synagogue, He healed a man who had an evil spirit."

Benjamin handed round the freshly baked bread which they dipped in olive oil. Rachel brought some olives and cheese for them to eat while the food was cooking.

When evening came word had spread round the village that Jesus had healed Peter's mother-in-law. So the people brought those who were sick to Peter's house. Jesus laid His hands on them all and they were healed.

"Come on you two," said Sarah lifting the bedding mats. "It's time for bed. Jesus is going to be busy all evening as the house is still full of people. We will need to sleep on the roof tonight."

Sarah and the children pushed their way through the crowd of people towards the door. As they made their way up the steps to the roof, Benjamin said, "Just look at all these sick people waiting around outside the house. It's as if the whole town has come here tonight."

"There are so many people needing Jesus' help," said Rachel looking at the crowd. "He will heal them all. Jesus won't turn anyone away, will He Mother?"

"No, Jesus will help them all," replied Sarah as they got to the roof.

"Do you think Jesus will get any sleep tonight?" asked Rachel sleepily as she lay down on her mat.

"He will probably only get a few hours rest, then He will be up early in the morning to pray to God, His Heavenly Father," said Sarah putting the blanket over Rachel.

"Well, it's been another busy and exciting day," said Benjamin lying down on his mat. "I wonder what will happen tomorrow."

Chapter Five – Jesus Heals More People

(Luke 17:11-19 & John 9: 1-7)

Every year Jesus and His disciples would go to Jerusalem for the Feast of the Passover. Sarah and the children, along with Mary and some other followers, would accompany Jesus on the journey there. They travelled South on foot passing through many towns and villages. Sometimes they spent the night in a field by the side of the road. Benjamin enjoyed sleeping out in the open under the stars but Rachel was a little afraid in case a wolf or wild dog came prowling around. Whenever they stopped for the night the children were sent off to find some wood to make a fire. Sarah would mix some flour and water to make the bread. Then they would all sit round the fire and talk while the meal was cooking. Rachel loved to sit near Jesus and listen to Him telling His disciples about God's kingdom.

One day, as they were going into a village, they noticed ten men who had leprosy, walking along the road towards them. The men hurried over to the far side of the road when Jesus and His followers came towards them.

"Jesus, Master, have pity on us!" they shouted. Rachel was afraid and hid behind her mother.

Everyone was surprised when Jesus spoke to them. "Go and show yourselves to the priests," He shouted over to them. Immediately the ten men hurried back to the village to see the priests.

Jesus continued slowly along the road to the village with the crowd following Him.

"Look, one of the men with leprosy is coming back," said Rachel in surprise.

"Praise the Lord, we have been healed," the man was shouting.

"Can he be healed already?" asked Benjamin as the man threw himself at Jesus' feet.

"Thank You, thank You, Master," said the man.

"Were there not ten of you who were cleansed? Where are the other nine?" Jesus asked. Then he said to the man, "Rise and go; your faith has made you well."

As the man left, Jesus spoke to the crowd, "Was it only this foreigner who returned and gave praise to God?"

"How do You know he is a foreigner, Jesus?" asked Rachel who was not afraid now that the man had gone.

"I am amazed that a Samaritan was the only one who came back to thank Me," said Jesus.

"Jesus knows everything, Rachel," said Benjamin angrily. "You didn't have to ask Him how He knew. Anyway you can tell by the clothes he is wearing."

"Come on you two," said Jesus kindly. "Let's get to Bethany where we can stay tonight. We need to get to Jerusalem tomorrow so we all need a good night's rest."

Bethany was a small village near the city where Jesus' friends Martha, Mary and their brother Lazarus lived.

The next day Sarah and the children went with Jesus into the city. Sarah needed to buy some food and Jesus and His disciples were going to the Temple. Soon a crowd of people were following Jesus on the way into Jerusalem. As they went along Rachel noticed a blind beggar sitting by the side of the road. He was holding out a small bowl and asking for money. When Jesus came up to the blind man James asked Him, "Who sinned, this man or his parents causing him to be born blind?"

"Yes, why was he born blind?" asked Rachel who felt sorry for the man.

"You are asking the wrong question," replied Jesus. "You are looking for someone to blame for his blindness. He is not blind because someone sinned." Turning to the crowd that was following Him, He said, "While I am in the world, I am the Light of the world."

Then Jesus spat on the ground, made some mud with His saliva and put the paste on the man's eyes. Rachel and Benjamin were surprised that Jesus did this but they said nothing.

"Go and wash in the Pool of Siloam," Jesus told the man. The blind beggar got up and reached out for someone to lead him.

"Can we help the blind man?" asked Rachel going up to him and taking his hand. She wanted to see if he would be able to see after washing in the Pool.

"Well, we pass the Pool on the way to the market, so I suppose we can take him there." replied Sarah. They had to walk down through the olive trees on the Mount of Olives and into Jerusalem by the gate near the Pool of Siloam. Jesus and His disciples went on to the Temple followed by the crowd while Sarah and the children took the blind man to the Pool of Siloam. As soon as the blind man had washed his face with the water in the Pool he shouted, "I can see, I can see!"

Some men who knew the blind beggar came over.

"How is it that your eyes are now opened?" they asked him.

"The man they call Jesus made some mud and put it on my eyes," said the beggar. "He told me to wash in the Pool of Siloam and I did. Now I can see."

"Where is this man?" someone asked.

The beggar looked about him, "I don't know," he replied. Then turning to the children he said, "Thank your friend Jesus for me."

"Can you really see?" Benjamin asked in surprise.

"Yes, I can see you and this Pool with all the people here," he replied happily. "I can make my own way home now," he said going off praising God for his healing.

"Come on children," said Sarah, "we must get to the market to buy some food for tonight's meal."

"Wow, we have just seen another miracle," said Rachel skipping along the narrow street. "I'm so glad Jesus made the beggar see. Now he won't need to sit by the side of the road every day hoping people will give him some money."

"Yes, I am happy for the beggar too," said Sarah with a laugh. "But he won't be a beggar now."

As they made their way through the crowded streets Rachel whispered to her brother, "I wouldn't like mud being put on my eyes though."

"Nor would I," said Benjamin, "I don't know why Jesus had to use His spit but it healed the man, so that is what matters."

Story 8 - Life on the Road with Jesus

Chapter One - Jesus Feeds the People

(Matthew 14:15-21; Mark 6: 30-44; Luke 9: 10-17and John 6:1-13)

James, Sarah and their children, Benjamin and Rachel, travelled with Jesus wherever He went. James was one of the twelve disciples Jesus had chosen to be His special helpers. As Jesus went around the countryside He told people the Good News that God loved them.

"When is Father coming back?" Rachel asked one day. "He's been away a long time with the other disciples. I miss him."

Sarah was grinding some wheat and Rachel was helping her by pouring the grain slowly into the middle of the millstones.

"I know you miss him," replied Sarah. "We miss them all but they are on a special mission that Jesus gave them to do."

"Rachel, you know that Jesus sent them out to preach about God's Kingdom," said Benjamin who was standing nearby watching them. "They had to go to all the villages with the Good News. Father is doing God's work."

"I know but I wish they would come back soon," replied Rachel sadly.

Just then Esther came running into the courtyard. She had been to the well to get some water.

"They're back," she shouted excitedly, "I've just seen Peter and the others coming down the road. Quick, make some bread as they will be hungry after their journey." Esther put her pot down on the ground and ran off to meet her husband and welcome the disciples back home.

"I wonder if Jesus is with them," said Rachel gathering up the flour around the millstones.

"We haven't seen Jesus for a few days now," replied Sarah. "I think He has been up in the hills praying to God, His Father."

"He'll have been praying that God was looking after Father and the other disciples while they were away," said Benjamin.

"Yes, Jesus would be praying for their safety," said Sarah putting some flour into a large wooden bowl. Then she poured some water into the bowl. Rachel and Benjamin watched their mother knead the dough.

"We will need to allow the dough to rise for a few hours," said Sarah covering the bowl with a cloth and placing it near the warm oven.

Later that evening Jesus came into the house wanting to hear how the disciples had got on. They were excited to report back what they had been doing.

"You have all done well," said Jesus. "You need to rest now. Come with Me tomorrow to a quiet place. We will leave early in the morning and take a boat over to Bethsaida away from the crowds. Sarah, will you and the children join us later? We will stay at Philip's house."

"Yes, I will come to look after You, Jesus," said Sarah. "I will make some more bread and buy some food at the market in the morning. Then we will meet You at Philip's house."

Early the following morning Jesus and His disciples left the house while it was still dark. Later that day Sarah and the children set off. After buying some food at the market they made their way down to the shore.

"Will Zebedee take us across?" asked Benjamin who always enjoyed a trip in the fishing boats.

"I'm sure he will. I'll ask him to take us over to Bethsaida," replied Sarah.

The children ran down to the water's edge where Zebedee's boat was pulled up on the beach.

"Where are you off to today?" asked Zebedee throwing his net into the boat.

"Will you take us over to Bethsaida, Zebedee?" asked Sarah. "We are meeting Jesus there. He has taken His disciples somewhere quiet for a rest."

"It's a secret," whispered Rachel. "Sometimes Jesus doesn't have time to eat you know."

Rachel climbed into the boat. She made her way to the prow, sat down and looked across the water. Benjamin followed her into the boat but sat at the stern.

"Welcome aboard," laughed Zebedee as he helped Sarah into the boat. He pushed the boat out into the water.

"Here Benjamin, catch the rope," he called out throwing the rope into the boat. When the boat began to float he too jumped in.

When they landed on the other side of the Sea of Galilee, Zebedee gave Sarah some fish and a handful of sardines which he had already cooked. Then he sailed back to Capernaum.

"Can we go and find Jesus?" asked Benjamin as they walked along the shore towards Bethsaida.

"Yes, you can go," replied Sarah. "Be careful, Jesus will probably be at a lonely, quiet spot. Here, take some food for yourselves. I know you will be hungry by the time you find Jesus."

Sarah wrapped up five barley loaves that she had bought at the market. Then she took two of the sardines Zebedee had given her and put them in the cloth with the bread. She put the lunch into the small basket Benjamin had tied round his waist. "Stay with your father and come back with him. He knows where Philip's home is," instructed Sarah as she went off to prepare a meal for them all when they got back.

The children hurried off along the path to look for Jesus and His disciples. After they had walked for some time Benjamin said, "Look, up there on the hillside, there's a large crowd of people. Do you think Jesus is among them?"

"I thought Jesus wanted to get away from all the people and there He is talking to them," said Rachel. "He loves people so much He just can't stop helping them, I suppose."

"Come on Rachel, let's hurry," said Benjamin running up the hill to where the crowd was standing around Jesus.

The children made their way through the crowd looking for their father. As they got near to Jesus and the disciples, Rachel overheard Philip saying, "Jesus we are out in the country and it's getting late. You had better send the people away to get some food."

"Where can we buy bread to feed all these people, Philip?" Jesus asked.

"We don't have enough money to buy food for ourselves far less for all these people, Jesus," Philip answered.

"We will need to send them to the village to get their own food." said Andrew who was standing next to Philip.

"There's no need to send them away Philip, you feed them," Jesus told him. Philip looked upset. How could he feed all these people?

Hearing this Rachel went up to Andrew. "We brought some food with us, Andrew. It's not much but you can have it," she said pushing Benjamin towards him. Benjamin opened the cloth and handed the basket to Andrew. Andrew thanked Benjamin, looked at the meagre meal, then took it to Jesus,

"Jesus, Benjamin has offered to share what he has," said Andrew, "but we won't be able to feed all these people with just five small barley loaves and two tiny fish!"

Jesus said to Andrew, "Make the people sit down."

Everyone sat down on the green grass. Rachel and Benjamin joined a group of women and children who were sitting behind Jesus. They watched Jesus take the loaves and pray, thanking God for the food. He broke the small loaves, then handed them to His disciples to give to the people.

"There will be nothing left for us," said Benjamin who was feeling very hungry.

"Just wait and see what happens," replied Rachel who hoped Jesus would do something special with their little meal. "Look, Jesus has broken up the fish too. He is handing bits of fish to Father and Philip to give to everyone."

After some time Andrew brought some bread to the children. Benjamin broke off a big piece and handed the rest to Rachel. After Rachel had taken some bread she passed it on to a little girl who was sitting beside her.

"Wow, how is there still enough bread for us all to have some?" Benjamin asked in surprise.

"And enough fish too," said Rachel as she noticed her father coming towards them with some fish in his hand.

"Ah! There you are," said James giving them some fish. "Andrew told me you gave your food to Jesus. That was very kind of you to share it with all these people."

"But how did Jesus make it enough for everyone to have some?" asked Benjamin. "I've counted over five thousand people here!"

"I think Jesus has just performed an amazing miracle," laughed James. "You can help us clear up what is left over after we have all eaten. Jesus wants nothing wasted."

"How can there be leftovers?" asked Rachel. Her father just smiled and continued to hand out the fish.

When the people had enough to eat and were satisfied they began to leave. Rachel and Benjamin helped the disciples pick up the bits of bread lying on the grass. Each disciple filled his wicker basket with the crumbs. Jesus told them all to go to the boat and head back across the Sea of Galilee. He stayed on the mountain alone.

"We will take the children back to your house Philip," said James as they made their way down the hillside. "Then we will take the boat as Jesus insisted we do."

"I thought we were to be having a rest here," said Philip. "We were to spend some quiet time with Jesus on our own."

"Someone must have seen us leave," replied Peter. "You know how quickly word gets around. The people must have followed us here."

"I can't wait to tell Mother what happened today," said Rachel as they arrived at Philip's house. "She won't believe that Jesus fed all these people with our little meal."

"We have learned something more about Jesus today," said James putting his hand on Philip's shoulder. "Who would have believed that Jesus cared so much for people that He didn't want to send them away hungry."

"The strange thing is I'm not hungry, even though I just had a bit of bread and some fish," said Benjamin.

"Benjamin, tell your mother there is a change of plan and Jesus wants us to go back to Capernaum. You need to sleep tonight and go back home tomorrow. I'll tell Zebedee to come over and get you in the morning," said James as he left the children at the door. "We need to get back to the shore and head for Capernaum tonight."

"What about Jesus?" asked Rachel, "How will He get back across the water if you take the boat?"

"He will return when He is ready," said their father, "He needs to be alone for a while to pray."

Chapter Two - The Storm at Sea

(Matthew 14: 22-27; Mark 6: 45 -53; John 6:16-21)

"I can't sleep," cried Rachel in the middle of the night. "What is that noise outside?"

"It's just the wind, Rachel," reassured her mother. "I think there is a storm blowing."

"What about Father and the other disciples out in the boat?" said Benjamin sleepily. He too had been wakened by the rain battering on the tiny window above where he was sleeping. Sarah cuddled up beside the children.

"Don't worry, Peter is a fisherman and he's used to storms at sea," she told them. "I'm sure they have often been out fishing when a storm has blown up. They know how to handle a boat when the sea is rough."

"What if Jesus is still on the mountain," said Rachel sadly. "He has not come back to Philip's house. He will get cold and wet."

"Oh, I'm sure He has found somewhere to shelter till the storm blows over," said Sarah trying to comfort her children.

"Will it still be stormy in the morning?" asked Rachel who didn't want to go in the boat if the sea was rough.

"We will see how it is in the morning," replied her mother. "If it is still blowing a gale Zebedee will wait till the storm is over. Now lie down and try to go to sleep."

The morning was bright and sunny with no sign of the storm that frightened the children the night before. Sarah took the children down to the shore where Zebedee was waiting for them to return to Capernaum. When they arrived home they found Jesus mending a window of Peter's house. Rachel ran up to Him and hugged Him. "Are You all right, Jesus?" she asked. "We were frightened by the storm last night."

"Yes Rachel we are all safe, but it was quite a storm," said Jesus putting His arm around her. "The wind blew the wood off the window but I am fixing it."

Sarah and the children rushed into the house to see if James was alright.

"You'll never believe what happened last night," said James as they all sat down to eat their meal.

"Were you afraid in the storm, Father?" asked Rachel. "Tell us all about it, please."

"Even I was afraid," laughed Peter taking some bread to clean his plate.

"When we left you at Philip's house," began James, "The sea was quite calm so we set off across the water. We were maybe about three or four miles out when a strong wind began to blow causing huge waves to come over the side of the boat. We tried to row the boat but we couldn't make any headway."

"With great difficulty I managed to pull down the sail," interrupted

Peter, "but it kept blowing away and hitting my face. It was pouring with rain and I could hardly see."

"We've been in storms before," said Andrew, "but nothing like this one. We were all terrified, scared out of our wits."

"In fact we thought that the boat was going to sink," said John, "and we would all drown."

"What happened next?" asked Rachel. She couldn't eat her soup till she had heard all about this scary adventure.

"Well, we thought we were about to die when we saw this ghost walking on the water," continued James. "We were so afraid we were actually shaking with fear. Then we heard Jesus' voice telling us not to be afraid."

"Was it really Jesus?" interrupted Rachel.

"Yes, it was Me Rachel," said Jesus calmly as He came and sat down beside her. "I saw the boat tossing about in the huge waves and knew that My disciples were struggling to keep the boat afloat. So I came to help them."

"We couldn't believe it was You Jesus," said Philip. "We had left You on the mountain."

"I hope you took Jesus into the boat," said Benjamin.

"Of course we did Benjamin. As soon as we helped Jesus into the boat the wind dropped and the sea was calm once more," continued James.

"The next thing we knew was that we had arrived safely on the shore right beside the house," said Peter.

"Wow," said Rachel and Benjamin together. "That's amazing."

Chapter Three - Some Stories Jesus Told

(Luke 10:25-37, 15:3-31 and Matthew 18:10-14).

One evening James and his family were sitting in the courtyard of Peter's house, discussing some of the stories Jesus had been telling the crowd. Jesus, Matthew and Thomas arrived tired and hungry. The children ran up to Jesus and took His hands. They brought Him to a comfy cushion that they had ready for Him and sat down beside Him. Jesus joined in the conversation as they waited for the meal.

"I didn't understand the story You told about the Samaritan, Jesus," said Rachel.

"What did you not understand, Rachel?" asked Jesus.

"Why did the Priest and the Levite not help the poor man who was attacked by the robbers? Why did they walk past him on the other side of the road?" she asked.

"Were they afraid they might be attacked too?" suggested Benjamin. "What do you think Father?"

"They probably would be frightened, Benjamin, but I think Jesus told this story to help us know who our neighbour is," replied James.

"Is that right, Jesus?" enquired Benjamin.

"Yes," said Jesus. "The religious man who asked the question about what he should do to have eternal life, just wanted to test Me. You know our Law tells us to help our neighbour. Well, he wanted to know who I thought was My neighbour."

"Who is our neighbour, Jesus?" asked Benjamin.

"Anyone who needs our help," said Rachel triumphantly, glad she remembered what Jesus had said.

"Yes, you are right, Rachel," replied Jesus. "The story was not about the Priest or the Levite, although they should have helped. It was about the Samaritan being a good neighbour."

"Why was a Samaritan a good neighbour?" asked Sarah handing some dates to Jesus. She hadn't heard this story so Rachel quickly explained to her mother about the man being attacked by robbers and left on the side of the road to die.

"A Priest and a Levite came past but they didn't stop to help the poor man," interrupted Benjamin.

"But a Samaritan came along the road and he stopped to help the man," continued Rachel.

"As you know Sarah, Jews don't like Samaritans," explained James. "So Jesus used a person who wouldn't be expected to help a Jew. Is that right Jesus?"

"Yes, that is right James," answered Jesus. "We have to help anyone in trouble whoever they are, even people we don't like."

"Jesus, You always help those who are in need," said Rachel.

"Yes, Jesus is showing us how to be like Him," said James.

Rachel followed Sarah over to the other side of the courtyard to get the bread.

"It's hard to be like Jesus sometimes," she said as she watched her mother take some dough and pat it into a circle.

"Yes, it is hard," replied her mother, placing the flat bread on top of the hot bowl-shaped oven. "But we can always ask God to help us."

Sarah handed Rachel a basket to put the newly baked bread into. When the bread was ready, Rachel took it to everyone.

"I liked the story You told the other day about the lost son, Jesus," said Benjamin.

"What did you like about it?" asked Jesus.

"The bit about the father running to meet his son," replied Benjamin.

"I've never seen you run, Father!" said Rachel with a laugh as she handed the basket of bread to Thomas.

"No, I don't suppose you have Rachel," replied James. "Fathers don't usually run. I don't think many fathers would run to meet a son who had left home and squandered all his money."

"I liked that story too," said Thomas helping himself to some bread.

"Why did you like that story in particular?" asked Sarah as she brought over a big pot of food.

She placed the pot on the ground in the middle of the group.

Everyone helped themselves to the food. Then they all looked at Thomas waiting for him to answer.

"The story could have been about me," Thomas began. "When I was about 19 years old I didn't want to work for my father any more. We were always busy and had no time to have some fun in the city. I wanted to see what went on there. The more I thought about it the more I wanted to get away. So one day I stole some money from my father and ran off to the city. I had a great time there, just like the son in the story You told, Jesus. After a few months one of my father's servants found me and brought me back to our house."

"Was your father pleased to see you too?" asked Rachel.

"Oh no; quite the opposite," said Thomas. "He beat me and locked me up in a small dark room in the courtyard."

"Oh, how awful," said Benjamin sadly.

"Yes, it was awful," said Thomas with a sigh, "but I suppose I deserved it."

"The son who ran away in Your story Jesus, deserved to be punished too, didn't he?" asked Rachel.

"Yes, he did," Jesus replied, "but My story was about our loving and forgiving Father God. God doesn't want to punish people, but they do need to be sorry for what they had done wrong."

"That's why I liked Your story, Jesus," said Thomas. "My father punished me, then he sent me away saying I was not welcome in his house. He didn't forgive me. Do You think God will forgive me, Jesus? I'm sorry for what I did."

"Yes, God has forgiven you because you are sorry for stealing money from your father, but you need to make things right with your father too," replied Jesus.

"I will," promised Thomas taking some grapes from the bunch on the table. "I just wish my father would forgive me and want me back."

"This is the Good News I want to tell people," said Jesus. "God is waiting for those who are sorry and want to come back to Him."

After the meal Jesus and His disciples left the house. Rachel helped her mother clear up. As they were washing the plates, Rachel asked her mother, "What part of the story did you like?"

"Oh, I liked the fact that every day the father was watching and waiting for his son to return," replied Sarah. "What was your favourite part in the story, Rachel?"

"The party at the end because the father was so happy to have his son back," said Rachel smiling.

"I thought you would like that part of the story," said Sarah with a laugh. "You always like a party don't you, Rachel?"

Later that night when the children were ready to go to sleep, Sarah asked them, "Do you remember any other stories Jesus has told us?"

"Yes," said Rachel sitting on her mat, "There was one about a lost sheep."

"Yes, I liked that story too," said Benjamin. "A hundred sheep were a lot to count, yet when the shepherd realised that one was missing, he immediately went to look for the one that was lost."

"Then, when he found it, he put it on his shoulders and brought it back home," continued Rachel pretending to put a sheep on her shoulders. "They had a party too, to celebrate that he had found his lost sheep."

"I knew you wouldn't forget the bit about the party," laughed Benjamin.

"Jesus also told the story about a lady who lost one of the coins from her headdress," said Rachel. "She looked and looked for it till she found it."

"Have you ever lost one of your coins, Mother?" asked Benjamin touching her headdress.

"No, but I would be very sad if I did lose one. Each one is very precious to me," she answered.

"If you did lose one, you would light the lamp, take the brush and sweep the whole room, just like the lady in the story, wouldn't you, Mother?" asked Rachel.

"Yes, Rachel. I would lift all the mats and look under the pots till I found it," replied Sarah.

"Would you invite all your friends and neighbours to a party when you had found it?" asked Benjamin.

"I suppose I would," said Sarah, "and you would help with the party wouldn't you Rachel?"

"Oh yes, I like having a party," said Rachel lying down.

Just then James returned home and sat down beside the children.

"Who's having a party?" he asked.

"We were just talking about the stories Jesus told about being lost," Sarah answered.

"Do you know why Jesus told these stories?" asked James.

"Why?" asked Rachel who always wanted to know everything.

"Jesus was telling the Pharisees and the Teachers of the Law that God is happy when someone realises that they are lost to God because they have done something wrong or bad," explained James. "God accepts everyone; no one is so bad that they can't be forgiven if they say they are sorry for what they have done."

"Thomas said he is sorry," said Benjamin quietly.

"Do you think God is having a party for Thomas?" asked Rachel.

"Jesus did say that there would be great rejoicing in heaven when one sinner repents," said James.

"Now lie down and go to sleep," said Sarah covering the children with their blankets.

"Does God go and look for someone who is lost?" asked Rachel sleepily.

"Yes, God is like the shepherd who went to find his lost sheep," said James.

"Jesus said He was the Good Shepherd," said Rachel.

"We'll have another exciting adventure with Jesus tomorrow," said Benjamin quietly.

"I'm sure we will," replied Sarah.

Chapter Four – Jesus and the Children

(Matthew 19:13-15; Mark 10:13-16; and Luke 18:15-17)

The next morning, as soon as they had eaten some bread, cheese and dates, the children went to find Jesus.

"Have you seen Jesus?" Rachel asked her mother. "He said we could go with Him today."

"Jesus was up very early this morning," replied Sarah. "Your father and the other disciples went looking for Him some time ago. He is probably talking to the people along the shore by now."

"Can we go and look for Him?" asked Benjamin rubbing his eyes.

"I think you need to wash your face to waken yourself up before you go," said Sarah with a laugh.

The children quickly washed their faces and hurried out of the house to look for Jesus. They had wanted to see where Jesus went to pray but He had already gone. Now they would have to look for Him. A large crowd of women and children were making their way to the shore, so the children joined them. Sure enough when they got to a large grassy hill side beside the shore, there was Jesus talking to the crowd. The children tried to get near Him. People kept getting in their way as the mothers pushed through the crowd. Suddenly everyone stopped as they heard a voice yelling, "Go away! Can't you see Jesus is busy?"

Another voice shouted, "Get these children out of the way. People have come here to be healed."

People were pushing and shoving and everyone was trying to get near Jesus. Some of the children began to cry. Rachel and Benjamin were trying to get to the front of the crowd when they noticed Matthew and Thomas directing a queue of people waiting to see Jesus. They ran up to them followed by some of the children.

"What are all these children doing here?" Matthew asked Benjamin.

"They want to see Jesus, but they were told to go away," he replied.

"I'm sorry Benjamin but Jesus is too busy healing all these poor people. He hasn't time for children," explained Matthew trying to keep the mothers from getting any closer.

"He needs a rest," said Thomas ignoring the children and their mothers. "All these people, we'll never get home tonight. We need to get Jesus away from all of this."

Suddenly Rachel noticed Jesus walking towards them. She ran to meet Him.

"What's the matter Rachel?" Jesus asked as she began to cry.

"The children want to see you, Jesus," she cried, "but they were told to go away."

Jesus looked over at the crowd of people and saw all the mothers with their little children. He heard the crying.

"Don't send these children away," shouted Jesus angrily. "Don't stop the mothers bringing their children. Let the little children come to Me; don't push them away, for the Kingdom of God belongs to them too."

Jesus called the children over. At once the crowd moved away making room for the children to get closer to Jesus. He put His hands on them and prayed for them. The mothers held out their babies to Jesus and He took them in His arms. Then He said, "Unless you accept God's Kingdom as simply as a child does, you will never get in."

Jesus touched each child and blessed them. He spoke kindly to the mothers. After everyone had seen Jesus they all began to make their way home.

Sometime later Rachel and Benjamin found their father.

"Oh, there you are. I was wondering if you two would come today," said James. "What a busy day it has been. I'm glad it's time to go home."

"Did you see all the children, Father?" asked Benjamin as they started to walk home.

"Yes, I did," replied James, "but what was all the trouble about?"

"Some of the disciples wouldn't let the children see Jesus," said Rachel taking hold of her father's hand.

"Why did Matthew not want Jesus to meet the children?" asked Benjamin sadly. "It wasn't kind of him to send the children away."

Just then Matthew, Thomas and Peter joined James as they walked home.

"Benjamin was just telling me you wouldn't let some children come to see Jesus, Matthew," said James.

"We thought that Jesus was too busy healing and talking to the people," explained Thomas, "He didn't have time to see the children."

"Jesus was angry with us," Matthew told James.

"I know," said Peter, "He was very irate. I haven't seen Jesus angry. We were just trying to help. We didn't want Him to get too tired."

"Why do you think Jesus wanted the children to come to Him? It's not as if children are very important," wondered Matthew.

"Jesus was angry with you for pushing them away," said Benjamin crossly. "Jesus likes children, He says we are important."

"Yes," said James, "Jesus has always been pleased to see our children. He loves having them around. I suppose He just loves all people, including children."

"Especially children," said Rachel with a laugh.

"You may be right, Rachel," said Peter indignantly. "Jesus did say that unless we accept God's Kingdom with the simplicity of a little child we won't get in. I thought we, of all people, would be part of God's Kingdom. Haven't we left everything to follow Jesus?"

"Yes, we have left everything to follow Him, yet today He says little children are welcome too. Then He gets angry with us for sending some children away," complained Thomas.

Rachel and Benjamin listened as their father discussed the events of the day with Peter, Thomas and Matthew as they returned home.

When they went into the house the children were anxious to tell their mother all that had happened.

"You have had an exciting time today," said Sarah mixing some herbs with the olives. "Now we must eat, Jesus will be hungry after such a busy day."

At last Jesus could rest and enjoy a meal with His friends. As they ate together Jesus wanted to explain to His disciples why children were important.

"You don't understand about My Kingdom, do you?" Jesus asked His disciples. Benjamin was standing beside Jesus, so He put His arm around him and said, "Anyone who will not receive the Kingdom of God like this little child will never enter in. The mothers had come a long way to bring their children to see Me. How could I send them away? I love little children because they love and trust Me. Everyone who loves Me is welcome in My Kingdom. I was angry with you because you don't understand God's love. You wanted to keep the children away but I wanted them to come to Me."

"I knew Jesus would welcome the children," whispered Granny Ruth to Rachel. "He loves and cares for everyone."

Jesus enjoyed a quiet evening with His disciples explaining to them about His Kingdom and what God had called Him to do.

Story 9 - Jesus Shows His Love

Chapter One - Zacchaeus

(Luke 19:1-17)

"When are we going to get there, Father?" asked Rachel sitting down at the side of the road. She was tired, hot and thirsty.

"Will we stay in Jericho tonight?" asked Benjamin leaning against the trunk of a tree. He was hot and tired too. They had been walking all day with Jesus and His disciples.

"Jesus wants to get to Jerusalem," replied their father James, giving the children a drink of water. "But at this rate I think we will have to find somewhere to stay when we reach Jericho."

"It can't be far now," said Sarah taking the chance to rest too.

"I thought Jesus was just passing through Jericho," said Mary. "He is anxious to get to Jerusalem for the Passover."

"It's all the people we meet on the way," explained James. "Like these men He healed who had leprosy. Jesus wants to help them all. That is why it has taken us so long to get to Jerusalem today."

"Are we far from Jerusalem?" asked Rachel with a sigh.

"We certainly won't reach there tonight," said her father taking a drink too. "I will go and ask Jesus."

James came back a few minutes later with the news that they were nearly at Jericho and they would stay there for the night.

"Come on children," said Sarah helping Rachel to her feet, "it won't be long now."

One hour later Jesus and His group of followers arrived in Jericho. Jesus stopped to talk to the people gathered at the city gate, while some of His disciples went on ahead to look for a place to stay the night. Sarah and the children walked on through the narrow streets hoping to find somewhere to buy some flour and fish for the evening meal. As they walked through the busy town, Benjamin noticed two boys knocking over a table full of money. All the money scattered on the ground. Silver and bronze coins rolled away down the street. Benjamin and Rachel stood watching as a small, fat man chased after the two boys. Rachel followed the man to see if he caught the boys but they managed to slip away among a crowd of people buying fruit at the market stalls. Benjamin felt sorry for the man and wanted to help him by picking up the coins that were lying on the road, but he was afraid the man would come back and think he was stealing his money. So he decided to follow Rachel to see where she was going. Rachel ran through the people buying food from the various stalls hoping to find the boys among the crowd. Suddenly she stopped as she noticed the two boys hiding behind one of the market stalls, laughing. Benjamin stopped beside Rachel as she whispered, "Sh, listen to what they are saying."

"It's a wonder the old, fat man didn't knock himself out with the big gold chain he wears round his neck," laughed one of the boys. The other boy was still trying to catch his breath. He was bent over, leaning against one of the stalls, breathing deeply.

"I bet you that old tax collector is on his hands and knees right now picking up all his money," the boy continued. The boys couldn't stop laughing.

"We were just in time. I noticed the Roman soldier coming along the road to collect Zacchaeus' money," laughed the other boy after he got his breath back.

When Rachel and Benjamin returned to their mother, they couldn't believe their eyes when they saw her. There was the small, fat man crawling about on the ground gathering up his money and their mother was helping him! The Roman soldier standing beside the table didn't help. He just watched the tax collector scrambling about the ground trying to pick up all his money.

"One of these days I'll catch those boys," muttered the man to himself. "I'll just have to charge their parents more money next week. That's what I'll do, maybe that will stop them making fun of me. I'll show David and Titus who is in charge here."

Rachel and Benjamin began to pick up the coins too. The man didn't seem to notice them. When he stood up to put the coins into a bag he bumped into Sarah.

"Oh sorry," he said in surprise, "I didn't notice you there."

"Here is some of your money," said Sarah handing him a handful of coins.

"Thank you. My name is Zacchaeus and these boys do this to me every week," said the tax collector. "I look out for them coming but they trick me every time."

"Here's some more of your money," said Rachel putting her handful of coins into a neat pile on the table.

Just then a crowd of people pushed passed Zacchaeus knocking over the pile of coins.

"Where are all these people going?" Zacchaeus asked Sarah as the crowd hurried by.

"It's Jesus," replied Sarah. "The people want to see Jesus. Come on children, we need to go now. Your father will be with Jesus."

Sarah and the children hurried off leaving Zacchaeus surrounded by people.

"Who's Jesus?" he called out to them.

"Haven't you heard? Jesus has come to Jericho. You know, the preacher who does miracles," someone told him. "Everyone wants to see Him heal the sick."

Zacchaeus wanted to see Jesus too, so he hurriedly gathered up all his money and put the coins into his bag. He handed the bag to the Roman soldier who was standing beside the table waiting for the tax collector's money. He then hurried along a back street hoping to get in front of the crowd. As he ran his big gold chain kept hitting his chin so he took it off and put it in his pocket. Suddenly he saw the people coming down the road. Zacchaeus wondered how he would be able to see Jesus as he was not big enough to look over the heads of the people. Noticing a tree near the roadside he carefully climbed up the tree making sure he didn't rip his fine clothes. From his vantage point he could see all the people making their way towards him.

"I'll get a good view from here," Zacchaeus said to himself. "No one will notice me up in the tree. I wonder what this Jesus is like."

The crowd was coming nearer. Among the crowd Zacchaeus noticed the two boys who had knocked over his table. He hoped they wouldn't see him in the tree. Lots of people were crowding round a man.

"That must be Jesus in the middle there," thought Zacchaeus.

As the crowd approached, Zacchaeus' heart began to beat faster. Jesus was nearly at his tree.

"Once they have all passed by I will climb down. No one will know I was here," Zacchaeus whispered to himself. "If David and Titus see me up this tree, they will laugh at me all the more."

Just as Jesus reached the tree He stopped, looked up into the tree and said, "Zacchaeus, come down immediately. I must stay at your house tonight."

Zacchaeus could not believe what he was hearing. Jesus had actually spoken to him. Without thinking Zacchaeus started to climb down from the tree.

"You don't want to go to his house, Jesus. He's a thief. He works for the Romans," said someone in the crowd.

"He's not an honest man, Jesus. Don't go with him. Nobody likes him," pleaded another man.

Zacchaeus didn't know what to do. Everyone was staring at him.

"Oh please come to my house Jesus," said Zacchaeus when he reached the bottom of the tree. "You are most welcome. I would be honoured to have You stay with me." Then Zacchaeus blurted out, "Bring all Your disciples too and these children," he added noticing Rachel and Benjamin standing beside Jesus.

"Yes, I am coming to your house now," Jesus answered turning away from the crowd. Everyone was amazed as Jesus and His disciples followed Zacchaeus.

"He's gone to be a guest of a sinner," said one of the bystanders.

"Imagine, Jesus going to Zacchaeus' house. He must know what kind of a man he is. You wouldn't see me go anywhere near a tax collector's house," said another man.

The crowd was very disappointed and began to move away. Nothing wonderful was going to happen. They had hoped Jesus would heal some of the sick people who had followed the crowd hoping to be healed. Now Jesus had gone off to have a meal with their chief tax collector.

David and Titus, being rather mischievous boys, decided to follow Jesus to Zacchaeus' house. Everyone else had gone off home but the boys wanted to see what Jesus would do.

"Jesus may change His mind and not go into Zacchaeus' house once He is there," said Titus.

"Maybe He will tell him off for being a tax collector," said David hopefully.

Zacchaeus had a large courtyard at the side of his house. When the two boys arrived, they realised they could just see over the wall. So they hid there, waiting to see what would happen. They watched the servants preparing a big table out in the courtyard. The party wouldn't begin for some time so the boys decided to go home but come back when everyone was enjoying the feast.

When they returned later in the evening they saw other tax collectors arriving at the house. Soon everyone was sitting round the table talking to Jesus as the servants served the meal. Suddenly Zacchaeus stood up.

"Master, here and now I give half my money to the poor, and if I have cheated anybody, I will pay back four times the amount," announced Zacchaeus.

There was a gasp of astonishment from the others round the table.

Jesus replied, "Today salvation has come to this house, because this man too is a son of Abraham. This is the reason the Son of Man has come. I have come to find and save the lost."

David and Titus couldn't believe what they had just heard.

"What did Jesus mean by "salvation has come to this house"?" asked Titus wondering what Jesus was talking about.

"I think He means that Zacchaeus is now a follower of this man Jesus too," answered David in amazement.

"Imagine, Zacchaeus being lost and now Jesus has found him," laughed Titus.

"What are you two doing here?" asked Benjamin sharply. The children had seen the two boys hiding behind the wall and had come out of the courtyard to find out what they were doing there.

"Who are you?" David asked in surprise.

"I'm Benjamin and this is my sister Rachel," answered Benjamin.

"We are friends of Jesus. We came into Jericho with Him today," explained Rachel.

"And we saw you knock over Zacchaeus's table," said Benjamin sternly.

"We were only having some fun with him," said David. "He takes our money and gives it to the Romans. We don't like him."

"Did you hear what Zacchaeus said?" asked Rachel.

"Yes, he promised to give back **four times** the amount of money he has cheated anyone out of," replied Titus.

"So that means Zacchaeus is a changed man now," explained Rachel.

"He is sorry for the bad things he has done and wants to pay back the money he took from people," added Benjamin.

"You may be right," said Titus, "I can't wait to tell my father."

"Yes, Jesus found Zacchaeus and now He is his friend," said Rachel.

"I bet Zacchaeus won't give us back what he owes us," shouted David as the boys ran home.

The next day Rachel and Benjamin were outside Zacchaeus' house waiting for Jesus, who had gone off early to pray. Some of the disciples had gone looking for Him. Mary and Sarah were packing up their belongings ready to leave.

"Will it take us long to get to Jerusalem?" Rachel asked Mary as she watched her put some food into her basket.

"No Rachel, it is not far to Jerusalem. We should reach there today," replied Mary. "Zacchaeus told me to take some food which was left over from the meal last night. We will stop at Bethany and share this with Martha and Mary."

"Will Lazarus be there too?" asked Benjamin hopefully.

"I'm sure he will," replied Mary, "Lazarus is a close friend of Jesus. He will want to talk with Him too."

Just then Sarah came out of the house to go to the well for some water.

"Now don't you two go running off somewhere. We are ready to leave as soon as Jesus comes back," she told the children.

Mary went into the house and Rachel and Benjamin kicked a stone to each other. Suddenly Zacchaeus came out of the house and hurried along the street.

"I wonder where he's going in such a hurry," said Benjamin.

"Let's go and find out," said Rachel gleefully.

Without thinking, the two children followed Zacchaeus. As they rounded the corner they saw David standing outside a house talking to Zacchaeus. Then they heard David shout, "Father, Father, look who's here. Zacchaeus wants to speak to you. I told you he wanted to give you back the money he owed you."

David's father appeared at the door of his house.

"What trouble has my son been up to this time?" he asked Zacchaeus.

"I have not come to complain about your boy but to give you back the money I owe you. Here it is," said Zacchaeus handing him a bag of money. David's father took the bag and weighed it in his hand.

"You will see it is all there and more," said Zacchaeus. "I have a note of everything I take from people. I got the job because I am good at keeping accounts. I'm sorry I stole from you."

"Well, thank you Zacchaeus," said David's father as he went back into his house.

"I must go and tell Titus about Zacchaeus," said David to himself as he ran off to find his friend. Rachel and Benjamin wanted to follow David but they decided they had better go back in case Jesus had returned and was ready to leave.

It was noon by the time Jesus and His disciples were ready to make the final journey to Jerusalem. As they were leaving Jericho, Benjamin saw Titus running up to them. When he reached Jesus he gasped, "Jesus, you won't believe what has just happened; Zacchaeus gave my father back his money."

"He gave David's father his money back too," Rachel told Jesus.

"I knew he would do what he promised," said Jesus with a laugh. "Come on, we must leave now."

"Jesus loves everyone, even those nobody else likes," Rachel explained to Titus.

"Jesus certainly is a loving person. I'm glad I met Him," replied Titus.

"I bet Zacchaeus is glad as well," shouted Benjamin as he began to walk away.

"We have to go now," said Rachel. "We are going to Jerusalem for the Feast of the Passover. Jesus wants to get there tonight."

The children said goodbye to their new friend and hurried after Jesus.

"Where have you two been?" asked Sarah when the children caught up with her.

"You'll not believe this," Rachel began excitedly. "Zacchaeus has given back all the money he owed, just as he promised he would."

"Remember the two boys who knocked over Zacchaeus' table yesterday?" said Benjamin. "Well, we met them this morning. That's where we've been. Zacchaeus gave back all the money he owed their fathers plus the extra he promised he would give back."

"That was good of him," said Sarah, "I felt sorry for Zacchaeus. I hope these boys won't trouble him again."

"No, they won't," said Rachel, "Zacchaeus is a changed man now. Jesus showed His love for him so he won't take more money than he has to. I'm sure he will give back the money to all the other people he stole from."

Jesus and His disciples set off on their way to Jerusalem with Mary, Sarah and the children.

Chapter Two – At Martha and Mary's Home

(Luke 10:38-42)

The sun was just setting as Jesus and His disciples arrived in Bethany. They went straight to Martha and Mary's house, where Martha welcomed them all and brought water to wash their feet. They were so pleased to see their friend Jesus. Lazarus came hurrying into the house when he heard that Jesus had arrived. He sat down beside Jesus. Mary sat at Jesus' feet wanting to hear all that He had to tell them. Sarah and Jesus' mother were also tired, so were glad to sit and listen to Jesus too. Rachel sat down beside her mother, put her head on Sarah's lap and shut her eyes. It had been a long, hot day and everyone was tired.

Suddenly Martha came in from the courtyard, hot and flustered.

"Lord, don't You care that my sister has left me to do all the work by myself?" Martha asked Jesus. "Tell her to help me!" she added angrily.

Rachel woke up with a start and Sarah got up to go and help.

"Sorry Martha," said Sarah quietly. "We should be helping you. We were just having a much needed rest."

"It's not you who should be helping me," said Martha crossly. "Mary should be helping instead of sitting at Jesus' feet all evening."

"Martha, Martha," said Jesus kindly, "you are worried and upset about many things, but only one thing is needed and that is what Mary has chosen. Listening to My teaching is far better than fussing about."

Rachel followed Sarah and Martha out into the courtyard leaving Mary still listening to Jesus.

"We will help you Martha," said Sarah picking up the bowl of flour. "Rachel, you can pour the water into the flour while I mix it."

"Can I put the bread onto the fire, Martha?" Rachel asked.

"Of course you can Rachel but be careful, it's very hot," said Martha calmly. "Thank you for helping. I'm sorry I was rude. It was just that I had so much to do preparing the meal all by myself."

"Don't worry, I'm sure Jesus understands," said Sarah mixing up the dough.

Benjamin came into the courtyard and asked, "Do you need me to run to the well for some water, Martha?"

"Oh thank you. That would be a great help. We always need more water," replied Martha stirring the pot of food which was on the fire.

After the meal, everyone including Martha, sat and listened to Jesus. Mary had promised to clear up all the dishes later when everyone had gone to sleep.

"I like staying with Martha and Mary," said Rachel sleepily as they all settled down.

"Yes, they are kind people and love having us stay with them when Jesus comes to Jerusalem each year," said Sarah lying down on her mat.

"Poor Martha, she was so distracted with all she had to do that she didn't have much time to listen to Jesus," said Rachel.

"That's the problem sometimes," replied Sarah. "We are too busy to stop and just be with Jesus. That is what He wants."

"I know," said Benjamin quietly. "Jesus just wants us to listen to His teaching and do what He tells us to do."

"Time to sleep now," said Sarah. "I think we will just stay with Martha and Mary tomorrow and not go into Jerusalem. Your father and the disciples will be going with Jesus to the Temple so we can stay here and rest."

"I could help Lazarus in the fields tomorrow," suggested Benjamin.

"Can we help Lazarus, Mother?" asked Rachel. "I could feed the chickens and the goats."

"Yes, I'm sure Lazarus would like you to help him," said Sarah.

As Rachel lay down on her mat she said, "Jesus never gets a chance to rest does He?"

"That's why He is here, to tell everyone about God's Kingdom," said Benjamin. "I suppose He doesn't want to rest, He has so much to do."

"He wants to show His love to everyone," said Rachel. "He showed His love to both Martha and Mary today didn't He?"

"Yes He did and He loves all of us too," replied Sarah. "Now go to sleep."

Chapter Three - Jesus is Sad

(John 11:1-44)

A few days later Jesus decided to leave Jerusalem and go to a quieter place away from all the crowds. Sarah, the children and the other disciples went with Him. The next day, as Jesus was teaching His disciples, two messengers came up to Him.

"Lord, the one You love is sick," said one of the men.

"Martha and Mary sent us to tell you to come right away. Lazarus is very ill," said the other messenger.

When James heard this he hurried to the market to find Sarah.

"Sarah," he gasped when he found her, "something awful has happened. Lazarus is sick. You must take the children and go back to Bethany to Martha and Mary at once. Jesus loves Martha, Mary and Lazarus. Tell them we are coming."

James hurried back to see what Jesus planned to do. Sarah and the children got ready to leave.

"We have to go back to Bethany right away," Sarah tells the children. "Lazarus is ill and we need to go to Martha and Mary. It won't take long if we leave right away."

"What's wrong with Lazarus?" asked Benjamin sadly. "He was fine when we left."

"I don't know," replied Sarah. "Your father told me to go back and help Martha and Mary. The messengers just told Jesus that Lazarus was sick."

"Is Jesus coming too?" asked Rachel. "He will make His friend better, won't He?"

"I don't know if Jesus will come," said Sarah, quickly looking for some food to take back with them. She bought some fruit and spices and put them in her basket, then they hurried along the road.

When they arrived in Bethany, Sarah saw many people weeping in the street.

"Lazarus is dead," one of the women told Sarah. "We have come to comfort Martha and Mary."

The children began to cry. Lazarus was their friend too.

"Oh dear, Jesus is too late," wept Sarah. "Lazarus was well when we left him. I wonder what happened."

"I don't like the noise these women are making," said Rachel putting her hands over her ears.

"They loved Lazarus too," explained Sarah. "They are sad he has died, that is why they are crying."

"Can I go and find my friend Ruben later?" asked Benjamin who didn't want to be with the mourners.

"Yes, later," said Sarah as they hurried to the sisters' house.

Sarah greeted Martha and Mary. Martha said sadly, "If only Jesus had been here, our brother would not have died."

Rachel stayed in the house with the women while Benjamin went to look for his friend Ruben.

When Benjamin found his friend, Ruben asked, "What's the matter, Benjamin? You look sad."

"We came back to Bethany because we heard that Lazarus was sick," said Benjamin. "But when we got here they told us he had died. I had hoped Jesus would come when He got the news that Lazarus was ill."

"Lazarus died three days ago and they have already buried him in the tomb," replied Ruben.

"If Jesus hasn't come by tonight I am going to look for Him tomorrow," said Benjamin.

"I'll come with you," said Ruben. "Meet me here tomorrow morning and let me know if Jesus has come. If He's not arrived in Bethany, we can go and look for Him."

The boys agreed to meet the following morning, then went off to throw some stones into the nearby stream.

Early the next morning Benjamin went to find his friend to tell him that Jesus still hadn't come. After he left, however, word came that Jesus was on His way to Bethany. When Martha heard this she hurried out of the house. She walked towards the end of the village looking for Jesus. Ruben was waiting for his friend and saw Martha walking along the road. Her head was down so she didn't notice Ruben. Just then Benjamin came along the road.

"Benjamin, I've just seen Martha walking past on her way out of the village," said Ruben when the boys met. "Quick, we can follow her and see where she is going. She's probably going to the tomb where they laid Lazarus the other day."

"You may be right or else she is going to see if Jesus is coming," said Benjamin.

"I know where the tomb is. Come on, if we climb that hill over there, we can see right down the road. No one will see us up there," suggested Ruben.

Benjamin clambered up the hill behind Ruben. When he reached the top he sat down because he was out of breath. From the top of the hill he could see some people below. Ruben lay on the ground looking down at the road.

"Why are all these people here?" asked Benjamin lying on his tummy beside his friend.

"I think they are here to visit Martha and Mary and weep at the tomb," said Ruben.

"I'm sure Jesus will come. Maybe Martha has heard that He is coming," said Benjamin.

"Why did He not come right away?" asked Ruben sadly. "I don't think Jesus will bother to come now. He will have heard that Lazarus has died."

"Jesus knew that Lazarus was sick, but I don't think He knows he has died," said Benjamin.

"Look, there is Martha waiting by the side of the road," said Ruben pointing to a lonely figure standing on the pathway leading from the village.

"Martha and Mary haven't stopped crying," Benjamin told Ruben. "I even heard them crying all through the night."

"The whole village has been crying for days, Benjamin," said Ruben. "Everyone loved Lazarus."

Suddenly a crowd of people came along the road.

"Oh! Look over there. They're coming. I can see Father with Jesus and Peter," shouted Benjamin excitedly pointing towards the crowd.

"It,… it does look like Jesus," said Ruben quietly. "See, Martha is talking to Him."

"I knew He would come," said Benjamin happily.

"Keep down, we mustn't let anyone see us," whispered Ruben.

The boys lay on the ground, quietly watching what was going on down below them. They could hear the people talking.

"Lord," Martha said to Jesus, "if You had been here, my brother would not have died. But I know even now that whatever You ask God, He will grant You."

Jesus said to her, "Your brother will rise again."

The boys heard Jesus tell Martha that He is the resurrection and the life and if anyone believes in Him they will never die. They were surprised to hear Martha say that she knew that Jesus is the Christ, the Son of God. The two boys noticed Martha moving away from Jesus so they crept down the hill to where some people were standing watching Martha walking quickly along the path leading back to the village. There was a large tree beside the road.

"Let's climb up into the tree while everyone is looking the other way," suggested Ruben grabbing hold of one of the branches and pulling himself up into the tree. Benjamin followed quickly and sat between two branches. After some time they saw Mary coming from the village in front of a crowd of people hurrying towards Jesus.

"We can get a good view from here and we can hear what is being said," whispered Ruben getting comfortable on a branch beside Benjamin.

"I don't think we need to whisper, Ruben," said Benjamin, "the crowd is making such a noise, crying and wailing that no one will hear us."

Mary ran up to Jesus and fell at His feet.

"Lord, if You had been here my brother would not have died," they heard her say.

The boys sat quietly in the tree listening.

"Where have you laid him?" they heard Jesus ask sadly.

"Come and see, Lord," said a man in the crowd.

"Look, Jesus is crying too," said Benjamin in surprise.

"Lazarus was His friend. Jesus is sad that His friend has died," said Ruben sniffing back his tears.

They heard the people talking about how Jesus loved Lazarus, yet He hadn't come in time to save him. The boys watched the crowd follow Jesus to Lazarus' tomb. When everyone had gone to the tomb, Ruben and Benjamin jumped down from the tree. Ruben knew another way to get to the other side of the tomb, so Benjamin followed his friend. They noticed a rock near the tomb.

"Let's hide behind that rock over there," whispered Benjamin crawling on his hands and knees so that no one would see him.

The boys quietly hid behind the rock. They had a good view of the tomb and the people. Jesus was standing quietly by the tomb weeping. The crowd suddenly became quiet. Only a few murmuring noises could be heard. A large stone lay across the entrance.

Suddenly Jesus said in a loud voice, "Take away the stone."

"What did Jesus say?" asked Benjamin in amazement.

"He told them to take away the stone!" replied Ruben in a whisper.

"They can't do that, there will be a stink," said Benjamin.

"I know; the body has been in the tomb for days. What are they doing? Oh no! I can't look," said Ruben.

Ruben and Benjamin covered their eyes with their hands.

"But Lord, by this time there will be a bad smell, he's been dead four days," they heard Martha say.

When Ruben heard Martha speaking he took his hands from his face. He heard Jesus saying to Martha that if she believed she would see the glory of God. Then Jesus again told the men standing nearby to roll the stone away.

"Oh no, they *are* moving the stone. Two men are pushing it away," said Benjamin unable to believe what he was seeing. "I don't want to look but I can't miss this. Will Jesus go in or will a body come out? Oh dear, this is awful."

The crowd was silent. No one moved as they watched in amazement. A crunching noise filled the air as the stone began to move. When the men stopped pushing, the stone rolled to a stop. Not a sound was heard. All eyes were fixed on the dark hole.

"Listen," whispered Benjamin. "Jesus is praying to God!"

They heard Him say, "Thank You God for listening to Me. May these people here believe that You, Father God, have sent Me."

Then Jesus shouted, "Lazarus, come out!"

"Jesus has told Lazarus to come out!" said Ruben in surprise, his voice trembling. "I can't look. What's happening?" said Benjamin afraid to look. Suddenly a body appeared at the mouth of the cave.

"Oh my goodness, it is a body, wrapped from head to foot in white linen clothes," whispered Ruben.

"Oh no, it's walking out of the tomb," screamed Benjamin.

"Shh, don't make such a noise, someone will hear you," said Ruben angrily. "Wait, Jesus is speaking."

"Take off the grave clothes and let him go," said Jesus quietly.

"Oh dear they are taking off the grave clothes. I wonder what his face will look like," said Benjamin peering through his fingers which were covering his face.

"Is it all horrible and eaten away?" asked Benjamin after some time.

"No! Look, it *is* Lazarus. He's just the same. His face is ok and he's smiling at Jesus," said Ruben.

Ruben got up and started to run towards the tomb.

"Wait for me Ruben," shouted Benjamin following his friend to where Jesus and the crowd were standing.

"Lazarus! Lazarus is it really you? Are you all right?" Ruben gasped as he touched him.

Benjamin walked slowly up to Jesus. He was not sure what to say. He didn't know what to do.

"What are you doing out here Benjamin?" asked James crossly when he noticed Benjamin beside Jesus.

"I came to see what was going on. You remember my friend Ruben, don't you Father?" said Benjamin.

"You two should not be here," said James sternly, "But you have seen a great miracle today."

"I can't wait to tell Rachel all about it," said Benjamin as they began to walk home. "She'll be wishing she had been here too."

The crowd began to move away slowly, talking excitedly about what had happened.

Martha and Mary helped Lazarus home, each taking an arm. Jesus and James walked back with Benjamin and Ruben. The rest of the disciples followed behind them, amazed at what they had seen. When they arrived back at the village, Sarah and Rachel ran to meet them. Sarah couldn't believe her eyes when she saw Lazarus walking towards her. Benjamin told his mother and Rachel all that had happened.

"Well, Jesus certainly showed His love to Lazarus," said Rachel as she went into the house.

"And He showed His love for Martha and Mary by bringing their brother back to life," added Benjamin.

"Jesus showed His love for all of us today," said Sarah getting some flour out of a big barrel beside the door. "We will need to make some more bread for the party tonight."

"A party," shouted Rachel. "I love parties." Rachel ran over to where Jesus was sitting with Lazarus.

"Jesus, we're going to have a party tonight to celebrate You bringing Lazarus back to life again," said Rachel giving Jesus a big hug. "Thank You Jesus, You are amazing. I love You and from now on I am going to call You Master Wonderful."

Rachel and the young girls were sent to the well for more water while Sarah, Mary, Martha and Jesus' mother prepared the meal.

When the villagers arrived at Martha and Mary's house the party began. Everyone was happy, glad to celebrate the wonderful miracle Jesus had performed that day. Many of the people who had been with Mary now believed in Jesus. The women brought their food to share, others carried mats from their houses and the men brought some wine. Then the party began with praising God, singing and dancing. Jesus sat quietly beside His friend Lazarus. Together they watched the happy villagers celebrating the amazing power of God.

Story 10 - It Is Finished
Chapter One - The Happy Parade
(Matthew 21:1-11, Mark 11:1-10, Luke 19:29-44 and John 12:12-19.)

After Jesus brought Lazarus back to life He took His followers into the countryside where He could teach them away from the crowds. When it was time for the Passover Jesus went back to Bethany. The celebrations for the Passover lasted six days, and everyone was busy preparing for this special Feast. Jesus and His disciples were getting ready to go into Jerusalem. Jesus' mother Mary, Sarah and the children were going too. The route they would follow was from Bethany, through the Mount of Olives, then down the Kidron Valley and into Jerusalem. Crowds of people were also on their way to Jerusalem for the Feast of the Passover.

"Come on Benjamin, I'm ready to go," said Jesus, "I have a special job for you to do today."

"What is it Jesus?" asked Benjamin excitedly.

"You'll just have to wait and see," laughed Jesus.

Everyone was excited and happy as they joined the pilgrims on the road. As they approached a small village called Bethphage Jesus stopped and called to Benjamin, his father James and Thomas.

"This is the job I have for you Benjamin," Jesus said. "I want you to go with Thomas and your father to that village over there." Jesus pointed down the road. "Just before you go into the village, you will see a field, where a donkey is tied to the gate. Bring the donkey to Me," instructed Jesus.

"What if the owner shouts at us for taking his donkey?" asked Benjamin.

"Don't worry," replied Jesus. "Just say that the Lord needs it."

Sure enough, as they went along the track towards the village, there was a donkey tied up to a gate, with her foal beside her.

"Can I untie the donkey?" Benjamin asked his father as he went to pat it.

"Yes, Benjamin," answered his father. "You untie her and bring her here. You can lead her if you want."

Just as Benjamin was untying the donkey, the owner, who had been working in the field, came up and asked, "Why are you untying my donkey?"

"The Lord needs it," replied Thomas.

"The Master will return it shortly," James called out. The owner said nothing and went back to work. The little foal followed its mother. Benjamin brought the donkey with her foal to Jesus. Jesus took hold of the foal and prepared to get on it. When James realised that Jesus was going to ride on the foal he said, "Here, let me put my cloak on the foal's back before you sit on it, Jesus."

James took off his cloak and put it on the foal. The disciples put their

cloaks on the foal too, then James helped Jesus onto its back. Benjamin led the donkey so that the foal would follow its mother. As they began to walk along the path others joined them. Rachel ran to get some palm branches which she put on the ground in front of the donkey and foal. Many others did the same, while some people threw their cloaks on the ground. As the procession arrived at the Kidron Valley the people began to shout, "Blessed is the King who comes in the name of the Lord!" Some shouted, "Hosanna, Hosanna in the highest," while others quoted the Psalms singing, "Praise God. Peace in heaven and glory in the highest."

"Jesus is like a King coming into His Kingdom," said Rachel as she danced along the path with the other children all waving their palm branches.

"Yes, He is like a King," said Benjamin as he proudly led the donkey. Turning to look at Jesus he added, "Jesus, they are giving You a royal welcome today."

"Why would Jesus ride on a lowly foal?" asked Judas as he watched the people cheering and singing while they climbed up from the Kidron Valley.

Matthew was surprised when Judas asked that question.

"Don't you know the Scriptures, Judas?" he asked. "The prophet Zechariah said that the Messiah would come as a King in triumph, humbly riding on a colt."

Judas said nothing.

"A young donkey is called a colt and it's an animal of peace," reminded

Matthew. "Jesus is coming in peace not as a warrior ready for a battle."

"Look, Jesus is going into Jerusalem through the Golden Gate!" exclaimed Peter as they arrived at the city wall.

As the procession entered the city many more people joined in the celebrations, singing and praising God. The crowd gave Jesus a wonderful royal welcome. Everyone was happy and the children were dancing and singing as they went along the narrow street still waving their palm branches. When Jesus arrived at the Temple, He got off the foal and went into the outer court.

"Benjamin, you will need to go with your mother," said James taking the rope from him. "Thomas and I will take the donkey back to the owner."

James and Thomas lead the donkey and her foal back out through the city gate. Sarah and the children went to the market to buy the bitter herbs and special food for the Passover meal.

"Can I go and visit my friend Mark?" asked Benjamin who didn't like shopping. Mark's father was a friend of Jesus and they visited Mark's home whenever they were in Jerusalem.

"We can all go and visit Mark and his family after I have bought all we need," explained Sarah. "It's too busy in the city today to go anywhere by yourself Benjamin."

After they had visited Mark's family, Sarah and the children started to walk back to Bethany.

"I'm glad we have Mark as our friend," said Benjamin as they went through the Olive Grove. "He's a bit older than I am so he can teach me the Torah. He helped me today to recite one of the prayers we say in the synagogue."

"Yes, it is good to learn from older friends," replied Sarah.

"Why can't girls go to the synagogue and learn too?" asked Rachel.

"I remember asking that same question when I was a girl," laughed Sarah. "Jesus' mother Mary reminded me that we can ask the men any questions we want to know about. That way we can learn too."

When they arrived at Martha and Mary's house, Jesus and His disciples were already there. They were sitting on cushions around a small table in the middle of the room. Lazarus was there too, talking to Jesus. Benjamin joined the men as they waited for the meal. Martha and Mary had been busy all day preparing the unleavened bread, boiled chicken and beans. When everything was ready the women served the food. After the meal Sarah sat down beside Jesus.

"Do You remember the first time we celebrated the Passover meal together when You were only twelve years old, Jesus?" she asked Him.

"Yes, I do Sarah," said Jesus reclining on a cushion. "It was My first visit to Jerusalem, apart from when I was a baby of course," He added with a smile.

"Tell us about it, Father," pleaded Rachel who loved to hear about how her parents had met Jesus when they were young.

"Our families would meet up at the crossroads before going into Jerusalem," began James with a smile. "I remember that Sarah's father, Simon, had decided to stay the night on the Mount of Olives as it was too crowded in Jerusalem. We young ones were very excited about camping among the olive trees and sleeping under the starry sky. The men went into Jerusalem to buy the lamb."

"It was your brother Reuben, who recognised My mother," continued Jesus. "I remember meeting you all that night. You invited us to share your Passover lamb. The next day I went with Reuben and James to the Temple."

"And we couldn't find You when we were ready to leave for home," interrupted Mary.

"I know, I remember feeling very upset that we hadn't looked after You, Jesus," said James sadly.

"Peter, do you know where Jesus was?" asked Rachel who liked this part of the story.

"Where?" asked Peter.

"Jesus was in the Temple talking to the priests and the Teachers of the Law!" replied Rachel.

"I should have known that Jesus would be there," laughed Peter.

Everyone enjoyed remembering when they were young and all the things that had happened since. Rachel and Benjamin loved to hear all about the past.

"Are You going to Jerusalem tomorrow, Jesus?" Martha asked as everyone got ready to sleep.

"Yes, Martha we will be going to the Temple as usual. Good night and thank you for a lovely meal," said Jesus as He went out to pray quietly by Himself.

Chapter Two - Jesus is Angry
(Mark 11:15-17 and Luke 19: 45-46)

The next day James set off with Jesus and the other disciples to go to Jerusalem. Sarah and the women busied themselves preparing and cooking the food. The children stayed in Bethany and went to look for their friend Ruben.

Later that evening when Jesus and His disciples returned from Jerusalem, Rachel noticed that they were all very quiet.

"What's wrong with Jesus?" Rachel asked her mother as she looked across at Jesus sitting by Himself in the courtyard.

"I don't know," replied Sarah. "He's had a busy day; perhaps He just needs to rest. Don't bother Him, I think He is worried about something."

Benjamin was going to ask Jesus to throw the ball for him to catch when Rachel whispered, "Jesus is upset tonight, so I don't think you should ask Him to play ball with you."

No one spoke during the meal and Jesus left as soon as He had eaten.

When everyone had gone to bed, Sarah spoke to her husband, "James, did something upset Jesus to-day?"

"Yes, Sarah, Jesus was very angry when we were in Jerusalem this morning," whispered James.

"What happened?" Sarah asked quietly.

"We went straight to the Temple as usual and entered the Court of the Gentiles," James began. "You know how busy it gets with all the pilgrims gathering there. At this time of the year the Temple is just a noisy, smelly market place. You've seen the merchants selling doves and lambs for the animal sacrifices and heard the money changers shouting their rate of exchange. Well, Jesus went up to the merchants who were selling the animals and began to throw them out of the Temple Court. He knocked over the tables of the money changers, scattering the coins all over the ground. He overturned the benches of those selling doves, breaking the cages. Doves were flying about everywhere."

"I wonder why He did that," said Sarah sadly.

"I don't know, Sarah," replied James. "Jesus then quoted the scriptures saying, 'My house will be called a house of prayer for all nations.' Then He told them that they had made it into a den of robbers."

Just then Sarah heard sobbing coming from the back of the room where the children were sleeping. She got up quietly and went over to see who was crying.

"What's the matter Rachel?" she asked gently when she realised that Rachel was awake.

"I overheard what Father was telling you about Jesus being angry and throwing everyone out of the Temple," she sobbed.

"Oh dear, we thought you were asleep," Sarah told her as she rocked Rachel in her arms. "You were not supposed to hear that."

"Why did Jesus do it?" asked Rachel between sobs.

"I suppose the Temple should be a quiet place where people can pray," Sarah tried to explained. James came over to Rachel to try and reassure her.

"These merchants cheat the pilgrims," James said quietly, "and the money changers charge too much for the special coins needed to pay the Temple tax."

"That would be why Jesus was angry with them," said Sarah covering Rachel with her blanket. "Don't worry about it. Jesus will be fine. You go to sleep now and you can talk to Jesus about it in the morning."

Rachel tried to sleep but she was sad because Jesus had been angry about what was going on in the Temple.

The next day Rachel asked Jesus why He was angry and upset. Jesus talked with Rachel reassuring her that it was alright to be angry when something was wrong. He told her He was fine and was going back to Jerusalem to teach the people.

Thursday was the day when the Passover was celebrated and Jesus wanted to share this special meal in Jerusalem with His disciples. So He told Peter and John to go into the city and look for a man carrying a water jar. They were to follow him to a house and prepare the upper room for their meal.

Jesus told Martha that He wouldn't be in Bethany for the Passover Meal.

"I have arranged to eat My last Passover with My disciples at Mark's house. Tonight is very important and I want to spend it with just the twelve of them," He said.

Rachel and Benjamin felt left out as everyone was busy preparing for the Feast. They were sad that Jesus and His disciples were not having their meal at Martha and Mary's house.

"Why can't we all be together as usual tonight?" asked Rachel sadly. "Sometimes Jesus just wants to be with His disciples," explained Sarah cutting up some vegetables. "You know that Jesus is doing God's work and nothing must stop Him from doing that."

"I know but I just like it when Jesus is around," replied Rachel.

"Jesus may not always be here Rachel," warned James as he got ready to leave for Jerusalem.

"Why do you say that?" asked Sarah putting the vegetables into a large bowl.

"I don't know," replied James, "but Jesus has been talking to us about leaving and going back to His Father. We don't understand what is happening but something has changed. Jesus is not the same, something is troubling Him."

Sarah and the children were upset at what James had told them. Jesus' mother, Mary, was also sad as she too knew something was worrying Jesus. Even Lazarus had noticed that Jesus was preoccupied.

"I'm wondering why Jesus said this would be His last Passover meal," said Martha. "I am really worried about Him too."

Chapter Three - Jesus is Afraid

(Mark 14:12-51)

"Benjamin, wake up!" shouted Mark banging on Martha's door. "Benjamin, Benjamin, wake up. Something awful has happened."

It was the middle of the night and Mark stood at the door, shivering in the cold night air. He was naked. He called to his friend again and at last the door creaked open and Benjamin appeared.

"Mark, what are you doing here?" he asked seeing his friend standing outside the door. "And where are your clothes? Quick, you'd better come in, but be quiet, the family is asleep."

Mark quickly squeezed through the open door, glad to be safely inside.

"Oh, you'll never believe what has happened," Mark gasped. "They've taken Jesus away. The soldiers came and arrested Him." Mark sat on the floor crying with his face in his hands.

Benjamin didn't understand what Mark was telling him. He brought a blanket from his bed.

"Wrap this blanket around you," he said handing it to him. "You must be cold being out in the middle of the night. Now come and sit over here and tell me what has happened."

Mark sat beside Benjamin and began to tell him the awful news.

"Well, as you know, it's Passover tonight. Jesus had arranged with my father that He and His disciples would come to our house to celebrate Passover there. Two of Jesus' disciples came in the afternoon to prepare everything. I was in bed by the time Jesus arrived with the rest of His disciples. I heard them going upstairs to our upper room. I listened to them talking for a while but I must have fallen asleep. Sometime later I was wakened by their singing. Then I heard the noise of them leaving. I don't know why, but I wanted to follow them to see where they were going. I quickly wrapped my bed sheet around me and crept out of the house. I hurried through the streets and saw them going past the Pool of Siloam and through the Fountain Gate. I followed them across the Kidron Valley to the Garden of Gethsemane. I was able to hide behind some olive bushes, so I heard Jesus tell His disciples to wait where they were while He went to pray. I heard Him ask Peter, John and John's brother James to go with Him. They went over to a rocky place a little further away. Jesus seemed really upset and told them that He was troubled and overwhelmed with sorrow. Then He told them to stay there and keep watch. I managed to get closer and saw Jesus go off by Himself, fall down on His knees and pray. It was as if He was weeping."

"Oh no! Jesus was weeping?" interrupted Benjamin. "He must have been very upset."

"Well, I can assure you Jesus was deeply distressed and troubled," continued Mark. "It was very quiet in the Garden so I could hear Jesus talking quite clearly. He was praying to God, His Father. I didn't understand what Jesus was saying. It was about not wanting to do something for His Father. Something about drinking a cup, but then He said He would do it if He had to. I was able to follow Him back to where His disciples were."

"Were you not scared they would see you?" asked Benjamin surprised at what his friend was telling him.

"No, everyone was too distracted about something else to worry if anyone was there. Anyway, as I was saying, Jesus went back to His disciples and, do you know what Benjamin? They had fallen asleep! Jesus asked Simon if he couldn't stay awake for one hour."

"Simon? Who's Simon?" interrupted Benjamin.

"Peter," said Mark exasperated at all the interruptions. "I heard Jesus calling him Simon, not Peter. Jesus was really sad when He realised that they had all fallen asleep. Mind you, I could hardly keep my eyes open, but I was so worried about Jesus. I wanted to go up to Him and tell Him to come back home with me and He would be safe in our house, but I knew I couldn't let Him know I was there. Jesus was really afraid of something, Benjamin. Three times He went off by Himself to pray and each time He came back to His disciples, they were asleep. I could make out the shapes of men lying on the ground."

"Was my father asleep too?" asked Benjamin sadly.

"Yes, they had all fallen asleep," replied Mark. "The third time He came back I saw Him wiping His brow. I'm sure He was sweating, although it was quite cool in the Garden."

"Why was Jesus afraid?" asked Benjamin quietly. "My father and the other disciples were with Him. Jesus was looking forward to sharing the Passover Meal with His disciples. I wonder what has happened."

There was a movement in the corner of the room and the boys stopped talking.

"Let's go up on the roof," whispered Benjamin. "We can't talk properly here and I don't want to wake up my mother."

Mark wrapped the blanket around him and the two boys slipped out of the house and ran up the stairs to the roof. Once settled in a corner by the wall, Mark continued his story.

"When Jesus went back to His disciples for the last time and found them still asleep, He woke them up and said, "Let's go. Here comes My betrayer.""

"Betrayer? Who would betray Jesus in the middle of the night?" asked Benjamin.

"You wouldn't believe who it was," said Mark. "Suddenly there was a light in the far corner of the Garden and I could hear footsteps. A crowd of people carrying lanterns, swords and clubs arrived. I could make out the temple guard and some soldiers too as the moon was shining brightly through the trees. And guess who was with them?"

"Who?" asked Benjamin.

"Judas!" answered Mark angrily. "One of Jesus' own disciples was in the crowd. I recognised Judas because he had paid my father for the Passover lamb. He went right up to Jesus and kissed Him. The men who were with Judas had swords and they stepped forward and grabbed Jesus. They were about to take Him away when Peter took out his sword. I knew it was Peter because of his size, he is so big. Do you know what he did?"

"I didn't know Peter had a sword. What did he do?" asked Benjamin hurriedly.

"He struck one of the men in the crowd, cutting off his ear. I could see the blood running down his face. The man, I think he could have been a servant of the High Priest, was holding his ear yelling and jumping about. I couldn't make out what Jesus was saying but I saw Him pick up something from the ground and touch the man's head. Immediately the man stopped yelling."

"What! Jesus healed someone who was going to arrest Him?" said Benjamin unable to believe what Mark was telling him.

"That's what Jesus did, but then all His disciples deserted Him and ran away. Jesus was left alone with the crowd and the soldiers."

"No! My father wouldn't run away and leave Jesus alone," said Benjamin angrily.

"Maybe he was afraid that he would be arrested too," said Mark. "It was very scary seeing the soldiers and guards carrying swords."

"Were you not afraid, Mark?" asked Benjamin.

"Yes I was, so I decided to get away as quickly as I could. Suddenly some men caught sight of me as I ran out from behind an olive bush. They grabbed hold of me but I managed to struggle free leaving my bed sheet behind. I just ran as fast as I could. It was only when I left the cover of the Mount of Olives that I realised I was naked! My heart was thumping and I felt sick. I didn't dare stop in case they were after me. That's why I came straight to Bethany. Martha's house is far enough away for no one to follow me."

The boys sat in silence for a while thinking over what had happened.

"I wonder what they will do with Jesus," said Benjamin after a while. "No wonder He was afraid. He probably knew what was going to happen. Jesus knows everything. But why would anyone want to arrest Him? He has never done anything wrong. Do you think the soldiers will let Him go?"

"It must be serious or they wouldn't have come in the middle of the night," replied Mark.

"I hope Jesus is all right," said Benjamin. Then he suddenly added, "Dare we go and find out?"

"Yes, let's go back to the Garden and see if any of the disciples are still there," said Mark excitedly.

"We might find your bed sheet on the way. They probably dropped it – it was no use to them," said Benjamin jumping to his feet, ready to go.

"Do you think we can help Jesus?" wondered Mark.

"I hope so. Come on, it will soon be light. Keep the blanket around you till we find your bed sheet. Then we can find out if Jesus has been set free," said Benjamin.

"Oh, I do hope they have let Him go," said Mark. "He was very troubled when He prayed to His Father."

"God will help Him," said Benjamin following his friend. They tiptoed down the stairs and hurried along the road that led to the city.

Neither boy spoke as they made their way back to Jerusalem. They were thinking about the awful events of the evening.

"What if God doesn't help Him? God wouldn't let them kill Jesus, would He?" gasped Mark as they reached the Garden of Gethsemane.

"Who said anything about killing Jesus? They will probably tell Him to stop teaching the people," said Benjamin. After a while he added, "But it would be awful if something bad like that did happen to Jesus."

The boys crept through the Garden. They came to a spot where the ground was trampled on and it was obvious there had been a lot of people there.

"This must be the place," said Mark looking at the ground. "See all the foot prints and look, the branches of these bushes are broken."

"Mark, look over there," whispered Benjamin, "there's your bed sheet on top of an olive bush. They must have thrown it away."

Benjamin ran over to the bush and jumped up to reach the white sheet dangling from a branch. He managed to catch it and handed it to Mark.

"I'm scared. I don't like being here," said Benjamin suddenly.

"I'm scared now too. You're right; there is nothing we can do. No one is here. Everyone must have run away because they were frightened," said Mark suddenly realising it was not such a good idea to be out in the dark, alone in the Garden. So they continued on their way to Mark's house. As they hurried through the olive trees and into the quiet streets of Jerusalem they wondered what lay ahead for Jesus, His disciples and for all who followed Him.

Story 11 - A Glorious Ending
Chapter One - The Awful Waiting
(Matthew 27:1-66; Mark 15:1-47; Luke 22:66-23:56 and
John 18:28-19:37)

Benjamin and Mark had decided to go to Mark's house to tell his father that Jesus had been arrested and taken away by some soldiers.

When they arrived at the house they discovered that the door was locked.

"Try knocking on the door," suggested Benjamin. "Perhaps they are still asleep."

Mark gave a gentle tap on the door. Nothing happened; no one came to the door.

"You'll need to knock louder," said Benjamin looking about to see if anyone was in the street who might see them standing there.

Mark banged on the door and shouted, "Father it's me, Mark. Let us in."

After some time a voice was heard from behind the closed door, "Who is it knocking at the door at this time of the morning?"

"It's Mark, Father, with my friend Benjamin," replied Mark.

The door opened slowly and a hand grabbed Mark. Benjamin quickly squeezed through the narrow opening before the door closed.

"What are you two doing out in the street so early in the morning," asked Mark's father, his voice trembling. The boys could see he was afraid and nervous. Just then James came forward and took hold of Benjamin angrily.

"You should not be here Benjamin. It's very dangerous," he said, scolding him sternly.

"We just wanted to know if Jesus is alright," said Benjamin starting to cry.

"I'm sorry to be cross with you, Benjamin, but something awful has occurred," his father tried to explain. "Jesus has been arrested and taken to the High Priest's house. We don't know what is happening. Peter went to see if he could find out what they were going to do with Jesus."

James wondered how the boys knew Jesus was in trouble but before he could ask Benjamin Mark's father said, "It's not safe for you to be here. The soldiers could come here at any moment and arrest all of us for knowing Jesus. Mark, you had better take Benjamin back to Bethany. Be careful that no one sees you leaving. We don't want anyone to know that this is the house where Jesus was."

"Judas knows," replied Mark, hurriedly getting dressed.

"What do you know about Judas?" questioned his father.

Mark told the disciples, who had gathered secretly in the house, all about what he had seen in the Garden.

"Mark, you must go at once and tell Jesus' mother, what has happened", his father told him.

"Benjamin, you must stay with your mother and sister at Martha's house till I come for you," instructed James. "Tell your mother not to go out or speak to anyone. No one must know that we are with Martha and Mary. It is too dangerous. Now go and be very careful," he warned.

Mark and Benjamin slipped out of the house and hurried back to Bethany. When they told everyone that Jesus had been arrested they all began to cry.

"I must go to my Son," said Mary. "I couldn't sleep last night as I had a strange feeling something awful was about to happen."

"My sister and I will come with you," said Martha. "It will not be safe for you to be alone in Jerusalem. "Lazarus, you must stay here with Sarah and the children. It would be too dangerous for you to be seen in Jerusalem after the miracle Jesus performed in bringing you back from the dead."

When the three women left the house, Benjamin told his mother, Lazarus and Rachel all that had happened that night. They were all frightened and anxious about Jesus. They were too upset to eat anything.

"It's become very dark all of a sudden," said Sarah noticing that the sun was no longer shining through the small window into the room. Their hiding place was now cold and gloomy.

"I'm scared," cried Rachel cuddling up to her mother as a loud crash of thunder shook the house. "I don't like it."

"Something awful is happening," said Lazarus looking out of the small window. "It seems as if the sun has stopped shining in the sky. It's pouring with rain outside and it feels as if an earthquake is taking place."

They waited and waited for word from Jerusalem. It would soon be the Sabbath which was the day of rest when no one did any work.

The children were asleep when Martha and Mary returned from Jerusalem. Jesus' mother Mary had stayed in Jerusalem. In the morning Martha told Sarah and the children that Jesus was dead. She was too upset to tell them how He had died. The women spent the Sabbath quietly preparing the spices to anoint Jesus' body. The whole room was filled with the smell of perfumes. Rachel helped her mother fold the yards of cloth ready to wrap Jesus' body in. For the first time she didn't ask any questions or ask why the women were doing what they were doing. Everyone was sad and when they spoke it was in whispers. When evening came only the children fell asleep.

During the night Rachel was wakened by the noise of someone moving about. She heard whispering then saw Martha and Mary quietly leave the house with the spices and cloth. They were carrying a small lamp so Rachel knew it was still dark outside.

By the time the sun rose Sarah had prepared some bread. Then she went to the well for water.

"Where have Martha and Mary gone?" asked Benjamin later that morning when he realised that no one was in the house except his mother, sister and Lazarus.

"They've gone to the tomb to anoint Jesus' body with the perfumes and spices," said Sarah sadly. "Now have some bread that I've just made. You haven't eaten for two days."

The smell of the freshly baked bread reminded the children that they were hungry. They ate breakfast out in the courtyard. Lazarus came and joined them. The sun was shining and the birds were singing on the rooftops. Although it was a bright, sunny day, they all felt sad and their hearts were heavy.

After everyone had eaten, Sarah milked the goat and poured the milk into the goatskin hanging between three sticks. She sat quietly in the shade of the courtyard pushing the goatskin full of milk backwards and forwards. As she was making the cheese she thought about all the things they had done together with Jesus. Tears ran down her cheeks as she remembered the fun and laughter Jesus had brought to His little band of followers. She also tried to remember when Jesus was serious and had tried to tell them difficult things like He was going back to His Father. Sarah just couldn't make sense of it all.

Suddenly, about noon Martha, Mary and some other women came into the house. They were all talking excitedly saying that Jesus wasn't dead. Mary Magdalene was with them and she couldn't wait to tell Sarah that she had spoken with Jesus. Even Lazarus could not believe what she was saying. The children were overjoyed at the news but were still not sure if it was true.

That evening they were sitting round the small table having something to eat when Mark appeared at the door.

"You're not going to believe this," he blurted out as he sat down beside them. "Jesus is alive and I saw Him in our house. The eleven disciples were still together in our house with the doors locked, when suddenly Jesus was there among us. He even spoke to us saying, "Peace be with you.""

"Wow, that's amazing," said Rachel jumping up and dancing round the room, shouting, "It's true, it's true. Jesus is alive."

"It all started early this morning," continued Mark excitedly, "when Mary Magdalene came to tell us that Jesus' body was not in the tomb. Peter and John didn't believe her so they decided to see for themselves. They ran to the tomb and Peter went in and saw the grave clothes lying where Jesus' body had been."

Mary Magdalene joined in excitedly, "I told the disciples that the stone had been rolled away," she said. "No one believed me when I told them the tomb was empty and that an angel told us Jesus had risen."

"Did you really see Jesus too?" Benjamin asked in surprise.

"Yes," she replied, "I was standing weeping beside the tomb when I noticed a man standing there. I thought He was the gardener, but when He said my name I knew it was Jesus."

"So Jesus is not dead," Benjamin repeated happily.

"No," said Mark, "Jesus is alive and I have seen Him too. I just had to come and tell you the good news."

"When is our father coming back?" asked Benjamin who wanted to hear the story from his father to make sure that what Mark told them was really true.

"You father will be back soon to bring you to my house," Mark told them. "Jesus wants all His disciples to wait in Jerusalem."

Everyone was overjoyed at the news, hoping that it was true. The children now knew that Jesus had been crucified on a cross but were not too upset about this because they knew He was alive again just like their friend Lazarus.

The following day James came to Bethany to take his family to Jerusalem to await Jesus' instructions.

"Do you think Jesus will come when we are at Mark's house?" asked Rachel who couldn't wait to see Jesus again.

"I'm sure He will," said her father. "But some people are saying that we stole the body and that we have made up the story about Jesus being alive."

"So how can you prove that it is true?" asked Sarah who was still trying to make sense of all that had happened.

"Well, what is interesting is that Peter noticed that the burial cloth that was around Jesus' head had been neatly folded up," replied James. "So that is proof that the body wasn't stolen from the tomb."

"How does that prove that the body wasn't stolen?" asked Benjamin.

"If someone was going to steal a body they would be in a hurry and they certainly wouldn't stop to fold up one piece of the grave clothes would they?" answered his father.

"That's true," said Sarah who was hoping to see Jesus for herself, then she would know Jesus was alive.

"Is Jesus' mother at Mark's house?" asked Rachel who realised that Mary had not returned to Bethany.

"Oh, did I not tell you," said James. "When Jesus was dying on the cross He asked John to take care of His mother. Mary is now with John."

"Wow, Jesus was showing His love for His mother even when He was dying," said Rachel.

"That is what we would expect Jesus to do, wouldn't we," replied Sarah.

"Come on children, it's time to say goodbye to Martha, Mary and Lazarus," said James, gathering up their belongings.

"I'll be sorry to leave Bethany," said Sarah. "It has been good to visit with our friends, but it will be exciting to be in Jerusalem for a while. I do pray that Jesus will show Himself to us too."

Chapter Two - Jesus is Alive

(John 21:1-25; Matthew 28:16-20.)

Jesus appeared several times to many of His followers, including Sarah and the children. While they were in Jerusalem, Jesus gave them His power - The Holy Spirit. Then Jesus told them to go back to Galilee where He would meet them again. So Peter and some of the other disciples went back to Capernaum along with James and his family. They waited for Jesus to appear again but He didn't come. They were still sad because they didn't know what to do without their leader, Jesus. Rachel and Benjamin were sad too. Although they had seen and spoken with Jesus once, they missed their friend and wanted to meet Him again. They didn't want to play with the other children, or go out of the house, in case Jesus returned. They didn't even talk much to each other. Benjamin didn't attend the synagogue school. Sarah felt sad and lonely too without her friend Jesus. Nobody wanted to do anything.

Late one afternoon as James and Andrew were sitting outside Peter's house they noticed Thomas, Philip and Nathanael coming along the road to Peter's house.

"What have you two been doing today?" asked Nathanael sitting down beside James.

"Nothing," replied James. "There seems to be no point in doing anything."

"We felt the same," said Philip. "So we decided to come and see what you were up to."

Just then Peter came out of his house.

"I'm going fishing," he announced to the others, walking off towards the shore.

"Wait for me," shouted Andrew. "I'm coming with you."

"Me too," said Philip, glad that someone had decided to do something at last.

"Good idea," replied James, "Let's all go fishing. It will give us something to do and hopefully we will catch some fish for our meal."

James hurried into the house to tell Sarah that they were all going out fishing.

"Could the children go with you, James?" asked Sarah. "They haven't been out of the house since we came back. It would do them good to be doing something again and Benjamin loves going out in the boat."

"I suppose they could," said James turning to the two sad children sitting in a corner of the room. "Would you like to come fishing with us?" he asked them.

"Go with your father, Benjamin," said Sarah, "I need to help Granny Ruth as she is not feeling well today. Even though she knows that Jesus is alive she is feeling very old and tired."

The children got up slowly and followed their father out of the house. As they were walking along the path by the sea they saw Zebedee painting their boat. James and John were helping their father.

"We're going fishing with Peter," Thomas called out to them. "Do you want to come too?"

"Good idea," said John, "we're nearly finished."

"Yes, on you go," said Zebedee. "I can finish the painting and hopefully it will cheer you up a bit." Peter and Andrew were already pushing the boat into the water by the time the others joined them. Peter threw his net into the boat then climbed aboard.

"Can we join you?" asked John helping Andrew push the boat out into deep water.

"The more the merrier," said Peter with a smile. "It will be just like before we met Jesus."

"Is it all right if the children come with us?" asked James lifting Rachel into the boat. "They won't get in the way." Benjamin climbed in after her.

"Welcome aboard Rachel and Benjamin," said Peter hauling up the sail. He fastened the rope tightly. By the time they were ready to go out to sea, the sun was setting behind the hills. Peter went over to Benjamin.

"If you want to be a fisherman you need to learn how to handle a boat, Benjamin," he said taking Benjamin by the arm and leading him to the tiller at the stern of the boat.

"There, see that headland over to the left, Benjamin," said Peter pointing out to sea. "Steer straight for that point."

Peter left Benjamin tightly gripping the tiller, while looking straight at the headland in front of him. Peter laughed to see how earnestly Benjamin tackled his new job.

"And as for you Rachel," said Peter putting his hand on her shoulder. "You can get us all something to drink while we get the nets ready. Andrew will show you where we keep everything."

When they were out in the middle of the Sea of Galilee, Andrew threw out the anchor. He tied the tiller with a rope and said to Benjamin, "You can rest now, Benjamin we will stay in this spot for a while."

Peter took off his outer garment and got down to work, throwing the net into the deep water.

The children soon fell asleep, rocked by the gentle movement of the boat. Later Peter hauled up the anchor and they sailed on round the lake looking for fish, but they caught nothing. As the sun began to flood the early morning sky with light, Andrew steered the boat towards the shore. Peter threw out the net one more time and left it floating aimlessly in the water. They all sat quietly staring into the sea.

"Can't even catch fish now," said Peter despondently.

"And that means no food for our meal tonight," said James sadly.

Peter pulled at the net one more time hoping they had managed to catch something. The net appeared out of the water with nothing in it. The others helped Peter haul the empty, wet net into the boat. As they drifted near the shore Peter noticed a dark shadowy figure standing at the water's edge.

"Friends, have you caught any fish?" a voice called out to them.

"No," they shouted back.

"Throw your net off the right side of the boat, and you will find some," said the man on the shore.

As Peter gathered up his net, the sudden movement of the boat woke the children. They watched as Peter and Andrew threw the net over the right side of the boat into the water.

"What's happening?" asked a sleepy Benjamin looking into the sea.

No one answered his question as they were too busy trying to haul in the net. It was so full of fish, that even with all the men helping, they could not get it into the boat.

"It's the Lord," said John quietly to Peter.

As soon as Peter heard this he put on his outer garment and jumped into the water.

"What's going on?" asked Rachel who always wanted to know everything.

"I think it's Jesus!" said Benjamin excitedly. "Just look at all these fish. It's a miracle."

Rachel looked over the edge of the boat into the water.

"Wow," she exclaimed when she saw all the fish swimming about in the net.

"It must be Jesus! They've caught hundreds of fish," said Rachel jumping up and down.

"It's just like the first time Jesus was in Peter's boat when they caught lots of fish. Do you remember that day, Rachel?" said Benjamin.

"Sit down Rachel," shouted James, "or you will capsize the boat. It's hard enough trying to get to shore towing all these fish without you making the boat rock."

Rachel sat down immediately but she was so excited to see Jesus that as soon as the boat reached the shore she jumped out and struggled through the water to Jesus. Jesus threw His arms around Rachel and lifted her into the air.

"Is it really You Jesus?" she asked through her tears.

"Yes it is I," said Jesus taking Rachel by the hand and leading her over to the fire He had made.

"Bring some of the fish you have just caught," Jesus shouted over to Peter who was standing beside his boat dripping wet. Peter climbed back into the boat and dragged the net ashore.

"Come and have breakfast," Jesus called to the others. "I have cooked some fish already and there is some bread too. You must be hungry after being out all night."

When they had all gathered round the fire, Jesus handed them some bread and fish. It was the best breakfast Rachel and Benjamin had ever tasted. They were so happy to be with Jesus again. Everyone enjoyed the food as they chatted with Jesus. After the wonderful breakfast James picked up two large fish saying, "I'll take these fish back to Sarah; she will be so excited to hear that You met us this morning, and I'd better take the children home too," he added with a laugh.

"I can't wait to tell Mother and Granny Ruth. This will make her feel better I'm sure," said Rachel.

Jesus walked slowly up the shore with James, Rachel and Benjamin, while the others removed all the fish from the net. Suddenly Jesus stopped and, turning to the children, said, "Rachel, Benjamin, I have something very difficult to tell you. I have to go back to heaven."

"I know you do, but you will come again soon won't you Jesus," interrupted Rachel.

"No, Rachel, that is what I am trying to tell you," said Jesus softly. "When I go back this time it is for ever. I have given the Holy Spirit to you all so it will be as if I am still with you."

"But I don't want You to go, Jesus," cried Rachel holding on to Jesus.

"I have to return to my Father, Rachel, so that the Holy Spirit can come to help everyone," explained Jesus. "You must be brave and not sad. You will know that I am with you always. I will never leave you or forsake you and I am leaving My Power with Peter, your father and My other disciples. Now go and tell your mother to meet Me here this evening. I need to talk to Peter as I have a special job for him to do."

The children hugged Jesus then hurried off home to tell their mother that Jesus had met them again.

That evening Sarah found Jesus walking by the side of the lake. They had a long talk together.

Later all eleven disciples went up the mountain to meet with Jesus for the last time. Jesus told them to go into all the world preaching the gospel, baptising all nations and teaching people to obey all that He had commanded them. Jesus promised that He would be with them always.

The next day James explained to the children that Jesus wanted the disciples to tell others about Him, His death and resurrection and His gift of the Holy Spirit.

"But I still miss Jesus," said Rachel sadly.

"I know, Rachel but Jesus doesn't want us to be sad," replied her father. "You can ask God to help you not to be sad and to understand what Jesus wants us to do."

"This is not going to be easy," said Sarah, "but with the help of the Holy Spirit we will carry out this amazing job for Jesus. God will help us when we face those who are against us and who will try to stop us telling others that He loves them."

"We will ask God for strength and courage to do this," said James.

"Then all who believe who Jesus is, will go to heaven too and be with God when they die," said Benjamin seriously.

"Yes, that is true, Benjamin," replied James, "we will go and preach the Good News of Jesus and it will spread all round the world."

Story 12 - Creation

Chapter One - Why?

(Genesis 1:1-3:24)

Rachel and Benjamin were sad that Jesus had gone back to heaven. They wished their friend Jesus was still with them. Although everyone missed Jesus, the disciples were excited that Jesus had given them the task of telling people who Jesus is, and that He is alive and wants to forgive and save people.

One day the children were playing in the courtyard waiting for their father James to return home. When he came in, they ran to greet him.

All of a sudden Rachel blurted out, "Why was Jesus born and why did He have to die on a cross?"

"Wow, these are big questions, Rachel," replied her father. "I think we need to go right back to the beginning to find the answer. Do you want to hear how it all began?"

"Oh, yes please, Father," said Rachel and Benjamin together.

"Well, it all began many thousands of years ago when God decided to create the universe," said James sitting on the ground. He leant against the wall of the house and Benjamin and Rachel sat down beside him ready for another exciting story.

"Benjamin, do you remember your teachers at Synagogue school telling you that there was nothing but darkness in the beginning?" James asked.

Benjamin nodded his head.

"Before the world came into existence there was just a huge expanse of darkness, nothing but darkness," explained their father. "So, when God decided to create His beautiful world He started with light. God had to make light first so that things could live on His earth. He separated the light from the darkness and named the light day and the darkness He called night. Then God separated the sky from the earth. Land and sea appeared. In order for the fruit trees, grass and plants to grow God made the sun to shine during the day…"

"And the moon and stars to light up the earth at night," interrupted Benjamin remembering what he had been taught.

"That's right," continued James. "Then a wonderful thing happened. God made fish that swam in the sea and He made birds that flew in the sky. God made huge whales and tiny sea creatures. He made big birds like the eagle and small birds like the sparrow. God was pleased with all He had made because everything was good. What is your favourite bird Rachel?"

"I like the dove," Rachel answered.

"And what about you, Benjamin, what fish do you like best?" asked his father.

"Oh, I like the huge whale," replied Benjamin, "I would like to see one."

"Did God make all the fish in Lake Galilee?" asked Rachel.

"Yes", replied her father, "all the different fish we find in the nets when Peter and Andrew bring in the fish."

"Stop interrupting Rachel," said Benjamin crossly. "I want to hear the rest of the story. I think I know what God made next, Father; the animals."

"Yes, God made all kinds of animals," continued James. "He made donkeys, cattle, reptiles, wild animals, dogs and cats, bugs and flies and every kind of insect."

As he spoke their father flung his arms wide open to show the children how big some animals are then he touched his finger and thumb together to show the size of a tiny ant.

"Even bears and lions and snakes and crocodiles!" added Benjamin in amazement.

"Why did God make spiders?" asked Rachel. "I'm scared of spiders."

"Everything God made has a purpose Rachel," answered her father. Before James could tell Rachel why spiders were good, Sarah came over with the food.

"Our meal is ready, Father can continue the story while we eat," said Sarah handing out the warm freshly baked bread. "I like to hear all about creation too. I think Father has come to the best part."

"What is the best part Father?" asked Rachel helping herself to some bread.

"Where was I?" said James, "Oh yes, God had made all the creatures.

The land was full of every kind of living thing. The sun gave heat and light. The water needed to make everything grow came from the rivers. Trees had delicious fruit, different plants produced seeds for the animals to eat, flowers blossomed and everything was perfect. But something was missing."

"What was missing?" enquired Rachel.

"People!" replied James, "God kept His best to the last – us! God made people just like Himself so that they could look after His world and take care of the land and the animals. People are to be responsible for the fish in the sea, the birds in the air and all the animals that roam the earth. God provided all the food His people would need. A variety of vegetables grew out of the ground as food for people, animals and the birds too. The flowers produced nectar for the bees and other insects. Some plants produced seeds to make bread. Trees and bushes had all kinds of fruit to eat. God was pleased with what He had created and it was all very good. It was a beautiful world and everything was as it was meant to be. That first couple were God's friends and He spoke with them. So long as they looked after His world and cared for it and obeyed what He told them to do, things went well. He wanted to be friends with His people and have a special relationship with them."

"That's a lovely story," said Rachel picking up a date and eating it. "So it all ended happily ever after."

"But that doesn't tell us why Jesus had to die on a cross," said Benjamin sadly.

"That's not the end of the story," said Sarah handing Benjamin the bowl of fruit.

"Sadly people didn't want to do what God wanted them to do," explained James. "They wanted to please themselves. They thought they knew better than God and wanted to do the things they liked to do."

"Our teacher told us that the first couple, Adam and Eve, disobeyed God and ate the fruit they were told not to eat," said Benjamin quickly wanting his father to know he had been listening to his teachers. "That's why they were put out of God's beautiful garden."

"That's right Benjamin, they disobeyed God, and were sent out into the world." continued James. "Then people became jealous, greedy and cruel. They spoiled the trees and the plants and killed the animals for food and clothing. They became angry and fought with each other. Some people were unkind and hurt other people. All this made God very sad. It was not how it was meant to be. All these bad things people did, God called sin. How could sinful people be His friends? They had spoiled the special relationship He had with them."

"Yes, I remember Jesus saying that people had sinned," said Rachel. "Remember the man who came through Peter's roof."

"Yes, there was such a mess," laughed Benjamin eating the grapes he had taken from the bowl of fruit.

"Jesus said his sins had been forgiven," continued Rachel. "So did that mean they were friends again?"

"It was not as simple as that Rachel," said her father. "If people are not sorry for the bad things they do, God has to punish them for disobeying His commandments. So how could He forgive people's sin and restore this friendship without punishing them?"

"He had a plan, didn't He?" said Sarah.

"Yes, He had a plan," said James quietly.

Rachel wanted to know what the plan was but she had to wait till evening as James had to go back to work.

Chapter Two - The Plan

(John 1:1-25 and John 3:16)

"I wonder what God's plan was," said Rachel as they went off to the shore to see if the fishermen were there mending their nets.

"It must be something to do with Jesus dying on the cross," replied Benjamin.

"Do you think God was punishing Jesus?" asked Rachel. "But why would He want to do that? Jesus didn't do anything wrong."

"You ask too many questions Rachel," said Benjamin. "I don't know why. Maybe there is no answer. Come on, there's Zebedee by his boat getting the nets ready for fishing tonight."

The children ran along the shore to where the boats were. After talking with Zebedee for a while they went to play among the rocks till it was time to go home.

It had been a very hot day, so when it was time for bed Sarah suggested that they could spend the night on the roof. They climbed the steps to the roof and Sarah laid the mats on the hard mud floor. The children were excited to be sleeping under the stars. They always liked it when they could sleep outside. When Benjamin saw his father coming up to the house he shouted to him that they were up on the roof.

James joined his family and sat down on his mat.

"Are you wanting to hear God's plan, children?" he asked crossing his legs.

"Yes," replied Rachel with a laugh. "We've been waiting all afternoon."

As the sun went down behind the hills Father began by asking, "Do you think God's plan worked? Do you think Jesus was part of God's plan?"

The children were silent as they were not sure about this plan. Then Benjamin spoke.

"Last week the Rabbi was reading from one of the scrolls that said they are still waiting for their Messiah to come," said Benjamin seriously.

"That's right, God had promised to send a Saviour. Our Scriptures called this person Messiah because He would save God's people from their sins," explained James.

"Jesus said He was the Messiah," said Rachel excitedly.

"Yes, Jesus is the person our people have been waiting for all these years," continued James. "God had promised long ago to send a Saviour, so He decided to come Himself, as a tiny baby."

"I saw Him just after He was born," Sarah reminded the children. "It was your Uncle Reuben who suggested that Mary and Joseph should stay the night in the cave next to our house. I still remember how tiny Jesus was."

"Then Mary, Joseph and Jesus stayed in your house didn't they Father?" said Benjamin who knew this part of the story off by heart.

"Yes, they stayed with us till they had to escape to Egypt," said James. "When it was safe to return, Joseph took Mary and Jesus back to Nazareth. As you know Jesus grew up and learnt about things just like we did. Joseph would have shown Him how to carve a piece of wood. Jesus went to the Synagogue school to learn to read and write just as you do Benjamin. He knew what it was like to be happy. He knew what it felt like to be sad."

"He probably hurt Himself playing," added Sarah, "Just like when you fell off the wall, Benjamin."

"Did He enjoy playing just like us?" asked Rachel lying down on her mat and looking up at the starry sky. "Jesus loved to see the stars and the moon they created."

"Don't forget all the planets in the universe," said Benjamin lying down and looking up at the sky above. "Our Rabbi said there are hundreds of other things in the sky too but we can't see them."

"Yes, God made everything and He knew what it was like to be a human being," said James. "As Jesus, He laughed and cried, ran about and climbed trees, made things out of wood and helped His mother. When He was thirty years old Jesus came to the River Jordan and that was where we met Him again, remember?"

"I remember how excited you were Mother, when you saw Jesus," said Rachel jumping up and down.

"That was when Jesus chose us to help Him," said James. "It was the start of His mission to tell others that God loved them. Jesus told the people how God wanted them to behave and how to care about other people. He showed them how to be kind and helpful. Jesus never did anything wrong but part of God's plan was that He should take the blame for what we do wrong. He was to take the punishment we deserved so that we could be His friends again. You see, some people didn't believe who Jesus is. They wanted to get rid of Him. Jesus knew they would crucify Him on a cross, and He accepted this as God's plan for our salvation."

"That's the bit I don't understand," said Rachel quietly. "If Jesus is God how could God want to be punished?"

It was dark now so Sarah lit the small oil lamp and placed it on the floor beside her.

"It is difficult," said Sarah softly. "Sometimes we don't fully understand but we just have to accept what Jesus told us."

"You see children," went on James, "God didn't kill someone else. **He** died so that we can be forgiven. However, as you know, because Jesus is God He came alive again so that He could show us who He really is. At first we didn't believe, remember. Now we do know who Jesus is. So we can start living the way God wants us to."

"The way God wanted in the beginning when He made His world," said Rachel. She thought for a while then added, "So that is why we need to know about Creation and sin and Jesus being born. He wants us to show people what it was supposed to be like."

"So that explains why Jesus came into our world and had to die," said Benjamin.

"We need to believe who Jesus is. We should want to follow Him and do what He wants us to do," said Sarah. "If we are sorry when we do wrong things then we will be forgiven and have eternal life."

"Don't forget that Jesus gave us His gift of the Holy Spirit to help us do what God wants us to do," said James.

"Now you and the other disciples have to carry on what Jesus began," said Benjamin thoughtfully.

Before the children went to sleep James prayed to God asking Him to help the children understand His plan for salvation. He prayed that he and the other disciples would be brave and go about the country telling others that God loves them.

*   *   *   *

For over two thousand years people have been hearing the Good News that Jesus loves them. The purpose and reason why Jesus was born into our world was for our redemption. God came as a real person to take away our sin. Jesus died on the cross so that when we are truly sorry, our sins will be forgiven. Everyone who believes that Jesus is the Son of God will have eternal life. So this amazing story goes on and on till all have heard about Jesus and His love for them. Then Jesus will return and God's Kingdom will have come as He promised it would.

Questions to go with the stories

These questions are for parents or teachers who are reading the stories to their children to help them interact and enjoy the stories. When you think over the questions for each story you will be amazed and excited about the truths it teaches you about God. You can read these stories in the Bible passages in each story. For children reading the stories for themselves, think over the questions for each story and try to answer them. These questions will help you interact with the story, making it more real, and you will find out more about Jesus.

Story One: The First Christmas

1. Which part of the story did you liked best?
2. What part of the story is the most important?
3. When was Jesus born?
4. How do you think the shepherds felt when the angels spoke to them? How would you feel if you met an angel?
5. Can you remember what the angels said about Jesus?
6. What were the names of the two people who met baby Jesus in the Temple?
7. Why do you think Jesus was born?

8.   Where was Jesus born? Can you remember the name of the town?

9.   Who do you think Jesus is?

10.   What other things do we do at Christmas time to remind us that Christmas is about the birth of Jesus?

Story Two: The Wise Men

1.   When do you think the bright star appear in the night sky?

2.   Where did the Wise Men come from?

3.   How old was Jesus when the Wise Men came to worship Him?

4.   What gifts would you have brought to Jesus?

5.   Why did the Wise Men go back by a different route?

6.   How did God tell Joseph to take Mary and Jesus to Egypt?

7.   Is there any part of this story that could be left out?

8.   Who do you think is the most important person in this story?

9.   Which person would you like to be in this story?

10.   Why did Sarah's family have to leave Bethlehem?

Story Three: A Special Occasion

1.   What was the special Feast Sarah and her family were going to?

2.   Where did this story take place?

3.   How old was Jesus in this story?

4.   Can you remember anything that Jesus saw in the Temple in Jerusalem?

5.   Why do you think Jesus stayed in the Temple after everyone had left?

6. Who was Jesus talking to in the Temple?

7. What have you learned about Jesus from this story?

8. When have you been on a long journey?

9. Have you ever been lost?

10. Which bit of the story did you not like?

Story Four: Baptism

1. What part of this story did you liked the best?

2. Do you know what being baptised means?

3. Why do you think Jesus wanted to be baptised?

4. Who spoke to Jesus after He was baptised.

5. What did the Voice say?

6. How do you think Jesus felt when He came out of the water?

7. Where did this story take place?

8. When did Jesus begin to tell people about God?

9. Have you been baptised or have you seen someone baptised?

Story Five: Jesus Chooses His twelve Disciples

1. Where did this story take place? Look at a map to see where this is.

2. When did the fishermen leave their boats after Jesus called them?

3. How did they catch so many fish?

4. What do you think Simon thought when he saw all the fish?

5. Whose name was changed by Jesus?

6. Why did Andrew say they were now fishing for people?

7. Why do you think Philip wanted his friend to meet Jesus?

8. What was Matthew's job?

9. Would you have chosen Matthew?

10. How many of the 12 disciples' names can you remember?

Story Six: The Happy Wedding

1. Who would you like to be in this story?

2. How do you think the bridegroom would have felt if he knew that there was no wine left?

3. What do you think Mary expected Jesus to do?

4. Did the children expect Jesus to do something special?

5. Why did the servants think that it would only be water in the 6 stone jars?

6. When did the servants realise that Jesus had changed the water into wine?

7. Where did this first miracle take place?

8. Can you keep a secret?

9. Have you ever felt embarrassed, annoyed or worried?

Story Seven: Jesus the Healer

1. How do you think the man with leprosy felt when Jesus touched him?

2. Was the Roman centurion afraid to come to Jesus and ask for help?

3.   Why do you think the Roman centurion didn't want Jesus to come to his house?

4.   When was the centurion's servant made well again?

5.   Why did Peter's mother-in-law get up right away to prepare the meal?

6.   What do you think about the four men breaking through the roof to get their friend to Jesus?

7.   Do you think the blind man would have been healed if he hadn't gone to the Pool as Jesus told him to?

8.   Have you been ill? How did you get better?

9.   Who does Jesus help?

10.   What have you learned about Jesus from this story?

Story Eight: Life on the Road with Jesus

1.   Which story did you like best?

2.   Would you have shared your lunch with Jesus?

3.   How would you have felt if you were in the boat in the middle of the storm?

4.   What part of the story about the son who ran away did you like best?

5.   Where was the son when his father saw him?

6.   Who has helped you when you felt left out or unhappy about something?

7.   When have you been sad?

8. Would you look everywhere for something precious that was lost?

9. Why do you think Jesus told the people about the lost sheep and the lost coin?

Story Nine: Jesus Shows His Love

1. Who do you like in this story?

2. Is there anyone that you don't like in these stories?

3. Why did David and Titus not like Zacchaeus?

4. How was Zacchaeus changed by Jesus showing His love to him?

5. Do you think the people in Jericho now tried to be friends with Zacchaeus?

6. Are you like Martha, busy all the time or Mary who wanted to listen to Jesus?

7. Why was Jesus crying at the tomb?

8. How would you have felt watching Lazarus coming out of the tomb?

9. What have you learned about Jesus from this story?

Story Ten: It is Finished

1. What part of this story did you like best?

2. Where did the children waved palm branches and danced along the street with Jesus?

3. Would you have joined in the happy parade?

4. Is there any part of the story you would leave out?

5. When was Jesus angry and why was He angry?

6. Why do you think Jesus had to pray to God when He was afraid in the Garden?

7. What made the disciples sad and upset?

8. Have you been afraid?

9. Who betrayed Jesus?

10. How do you think the children felt when they heard about Jesus being arrested?

Story Eleven: A Glorious ending

1. How would you have felt waiting for news about Jesus?

2. Do you think Jesus knew He was going to die?

3. When did Jesus rise from the grave?

4. Would you have believed that Jesus was alive again?

5. What feelings would you have had if you were in the upper room and Jesus suddenly appeared?

6. Where did Jesus have breakfast with the children and some of His disciples?

7. Who did Jesus send to help the disciples with the work they were to do?

8. What did Jesus tell the disciples to do?

9. Why did Jesus say He would not see the children or the disciples again?

10. Is there any part of this story you would leave out?

Story Twelve: Creation

1. Why did Jesus have to die on a cross?

2. What was God's plan for His people?

3. Can you remember the order that God created His world? What did He create first?

4. Where can you find all these stories?

5. When is Jesus coming back?

6. How did Sarah, James and the other disciples feel about the job Jesus gave them to do?

7. Who would help them?

8. How can we tell others that Jesus loves them?

9. Do you want to have a special relationship with Jesus?

10. What does it mean to you that Jesus is our Saviour, King, Friend and Creator of His universe?

A Journey with Jesus

A Journey with Jesus